基础会计

章之旺　付小雨　主编

中国纺织出版社有限公司

图书在版编目（CIP）数据

基础会计：英文 / 章之旺，付小雨主编 . -- 北京：中国纺织出版社有限公司，2024.11. -- ISBN 978-7 -5229-2255-3

Ⅰ . F230

中国国家版本馆 CIP 数据核字第 2024TU3513 号

责任编辑：郭　婷　韩　阳　　　责任校对：王蕙莹
责任印制：储志伟

中国纺织出版社有限公司出版发行
地址：北京市朝阳区百子湾东里A407号楼　邮政编码：100124
销售电话：010—67004422　传真：010—87155801
http://www.c-textilep.com
中国纺织出版社天猫旗舰店
官方微博 http://weibo.com/2119887771
天津千鹤文化传播有限公司印刷　各地新华书店经销
2024年11月第1版第1次印刷
开本：710×1000　1/16　印张：8.75
字数：150千字　定价：68.00元

前　言

目前，高等教育本科阶段的会计英语相关教材主要是引进国外的原版教材，或者只是参照西方的会计核算与财务处理方式，忽视了我国国情与学情分析，造成理论与实践脱节，影响了学生的学习兴趣与实际运用能力。与此同时，中国会计国际化进程正在加快，对会计从业人员的要求越来越高，因此，如何培养具有良好的外语能力及知识结构的国际化会计人才是我国高等会计教育所面临的一个紧迫课题。本书在编写过程中充分考虑国内三资企业对人才的实际需求，以会计英语的基本理论知识为立足点，以期帮助学生运用基础的专业英语完成英语环境中的会计实际工作任务。

本书共分为 7 章：第 1 章是总论；第 2 章是对会计核算基础和会计要素的叙述；第 3 至第 6 章是关于复式记账、会计凭证与会计账簿、会计循环账务处理、账项调整和结账的知识；第 7 章为错账的账务处理介绍。

作为会计学的入门教材——基础会计，本书具有以下特点：

1. 体系完整、结构合理、系统性强

本书主要以基础会计为体系，内容包括会计学原理中的基本概念、基本理论、平衡原理、记账机制、核算方法及会计报表等为各类初学会计的读者提供了最基本的会计知识。本书是财务会计的先导与基础部分，具有系统性、连续性、完整性的特点。

2. 继承务实、承上启下、推陈出新

本书虽然沿用了传统会计学的体系模式，但充分吸收当代西方会计，尤其是以美国为代表的国际会计研究的会计理论与实务方法，结合我国会计发展的具体实践，

有选择地组织符合我国国情的会计教材内容，去粗取精、中西结合，以较新的内容呈现给学生，使之更具现实性、国际化，以顺应会计国际化的发展趋势。

3. 通俗易懂、深入浅出、适用面广

本书基本素材参考原版教材，但表述形式力求符合中国人的思维习惯、价值观念与文化特征，深入浅出、通俗易懂，以适应不同层面学生的学习，既适合高等院校会计专业本专科学生使用，也可供其他专业学生及各类人员的选修自学之用。

本书由章之旺、付小雨主编，负责全书写作大纲的拟定和编写的组织工作，并总纂定稿。撰写初稿分工如下：第 1 、第 2 章由戴雪艳老师执笔；第 3 、第 4 、第 5 章由付小雨老师执笔；第 6 、第 7 章由章之旺教授执笔。在编写过程中，我们参考了国内外相关专家和学者的文献，并得到了实务界人士的支持与帮助。同时，本书是三江学院财务管理国家一流专业建设的成果，编写得到了三江学院法商学院领导的热情鼓励与大力支持。在此一并向诸位领导、专家及同仁致以诚挚的谢意。

编 者

2024 年 4 月

CONTENTS

Chapter 4　Accounting Vouchers and Accounting Books

Chapter 5　Main Business Transactions

Chapter 6　Adjusting Entries Before Closing Procedure

Chapter 7　Errors and Suspense Accounts

References

Chapter 1　Introduction

Learning Objectives:

(1) Understand the scarcity of resources.

(2) Understand the different sectors in the economy.

(3) Understand the main forms of business organization within the private sector.

(4) Understand the emergence and development of accounting.

(5) Understand how the ACCOUNTING EQUATION can be used and what it represents.

- Define accounting.
- Understand the functions of accounting.
- Describe the accounting process.
- Define the six main accounting elements.
- Construct the accounting equation.

1.1 Scarcity of Resources

Due to the scarcity of resources and people's possession of scarce resources, people have a demand for exchange. That means to exchange the resources you have for the resources you need but don't have. From barter in ancient times to currency as a form of settlement, it is because of exchange that we have the concept of "economy". The movement of resources (expressed in the form of funds) is recorded and reported in a certain form, so accounting is coming into being.

Accounting is the language of economy: Accounting is mainly to recognize, measure, record and report economic business. It has been said that accounting is the language of business. Every part of the business is affected by accounting. Management of a business depends on financial information in making sound operational decisions. Stockholders must have financial information in order to measure management's performance and to evaluate their holdings. Potential investors need financial data in order to compare prospective investments. Creditors must consider the financial strength of a business before permitting it to borrow funds. Also, many laws require that extensive financial information be reported to the various governmental agencies at least annually.

1.2 Sectors in the Economy

It is common to classify economic activities into two sections, the public sector and the private sector.

1.2.1 The Public Sector

The public sector is owned and controlled by the government. This covers all levels of government-from local to central government-and includes all the organizations which are funded by the taxpayers. The public sector is not as large as, 30 years ago, due to successive governments pursuing a policy of privatization, transferring organizations from the public to the private sector, but still accounts for a significant proportion of the business activity in the UK. Examples of public sections activities in the UK include the National Health services and the provision of libraries.

1.2.2 The Private Sector

The private sector consists of businesses owned and controlled by private individuals acting either on their own or in groups. Although private sector organizations have to comply with laws and regulations set out by the government, these businesses are free to pursue their own ends. It is business organizations within the private sections that this textbook will be exploring.

1.3 Types of Business Organizations

There are three main types of business organizations within the private sector.

1.3.1 Sole Trader/Sole Proprietor

• Owned by a person who assumes all risks for the business and makes all business decisions.

A sole trader is a one-person business (The business is owned by one person, but others can be employed to work within the business).

The sole trader is an unincorporated business organization. This means that the legal status of the business is no different from that of the owner. If the business cannot pay its debts then it would be up to the owners to clear the debts even if this means selling personal (non-ousiness) assets to clear the business debt. Sole traders are generally small organizations but are very common mainly due to the easiness of setting up as a sole trader.

1.3.2 Partnership

• Conducted in common by two or more people with a view to profit. They share the risks and decision-making.

Partnerships are also unincorporated businesses. Historically a partnership was owned by between two and 20 partners, although the limit on the maximum number of the partners was relaxed in 2002. A great number of owners potentially allow a greater contribution of capital into the business to increase the chances of success and minimize the risks of failure. However, partners may still have to sell their possessions to clear the debts of the partnership in certain circumstances.

A limited partnership is a variant on the partnership. This form of organization allows some (but not all) partners to enjoy limited liability, which means that they avoid the risk of selling personal possessions.

1.3.3 Limited Company

• Registered under Company Law.
• Capital is obtained from a number of people who buy shares in the company.
• Shareholders have limited liability.

The company has undergone the process of incorporation. This means a company exists separately from those who own the company. This means that the company will carry on business independently from the owners, and the owners of limited companies are known as shareholders.

There are two types of limited companys: public limited companies and private limited companies. They are run by directors elected by the shareholders.

It is appropriate to talk of a "separation of ownership from control". It is the shareholders who own the company. But it is the directors and managers who actually run the company. This can potentially cause a conflict of interest as the two groups may have differing objectives. This conflict highlights the importance of having clearly presented and understandable financial statements for user groups to examine and assess.

As stated above this textbook is probably concerned with the accounts of sole trader.

1.4 Business Objective

1.4.1 Profit Maximisation

The profit maximisation means to get the maximum income with the minimum investment and ensure that all transactions achieve the maximization of interests between customers and enterprises.

1.4.2 Shareholders' Proceeds Maximisation

Shareholders' proceeds maximisation refers to bringing the most wealth to shareholders through reasonable financial management. Scholars who hold this view believe that the purpose of shareholders' funding enterprises is to increase wealth. They are the owners of enterprises and the providers of enterprise capital. The value of their investment is that it can bring future rewards to the owners, including obtaining dividends and selling equity to obtain cash. Therefore, the maximization of shareholders' wealth is ultimately reflected in the stock price.

1.4.3 Stakeholders' Benefits Maximisation

Stakeholders' benefits maximisation refers to the maximization of the total value of the enterprise on the basis of ensuring the long-term stable development of the enterprise through the reasonable financial operation of the enterprise, the adoption of the optimal financial policies, and the full consideration of the time value of capital and the relationship between risk and reward. This goal puts the long-term stable development of enterprises in the first place, emphasize meeting the interests of all parties in the growth of enterprise value, is conducive to overcoming the problem of monitoring behavior of operators under the condition of asymmetric information, and ensures equality and independence among the subjects of enterprise governance structure.

1.5 The Relationship between Accounting and Business

There is a close relationship between enterprise accounting and enterprises. Enterprise accounting plays an important role in all business activities of enterprises. The main task of enterprise accounting is to make a budget and estimate for the macro and micro economic development of enterprises, and provide resource data information for the internal management of enterprises. The reliability and accuracy of financial information reflected by enterprise accounting directly affect the investment plan and financial relationship of enterprises. The work quality of enterprise accounting has a great impact on the economic activities and development of enterprises. Therefore, accounting control is the key to the success of enterprises.

1.6 Emergence and Development of Accounting

The emergence and development of accounting are generally divided into three stages: Ancient accounting stage, modern accounting stage and contemporary accounting stage. Before ancient accounting stage, there was a time called embryonic stage which was a pre-ancient time for accounting.

1.6.1 Embryonic stage

As we said before, the scarcity and monopoly of resources led to the emergence of exchange and gradually developed the economy. As early as the primitive society, when people hunted collectively and the daily supplies could produce a surplus, mankind began the act of accounting, that is, simple recording. With the emergence of recording and measuring behaviors, such as stone carving, stone counting, rope tying, etc., accounting began to sprout.

1.6.2 Ancient Accounting Stage

The division time of ancient accounting is generally recognized as the 11th century to the 15th century BC. At that time, the society was a slave society. During period of feudal society, professional accountants and accounting institutions appeared, and the term accounting also came into being.

For example:

In China's Zhou Dynasty, accounting institutions and specialized personnel were established; The term "accounting" also came into being in that period; At the same time, it also produced a certain accounting thought. For example, during the Spring and Autumn period and the Warring States period (771-221 BC), Mencius wrote: "Confucius tasted as a commissar and said: accounting is all that matters." This is the earliest thought and theory about accounting since China recorded it. The state of finance of the Zhou Dynasty was well organized.

1.6.3 Modern Accounting Stage

From the 15th century to the 1930s, it is the division time of modern accounting, and the main symbol is the birth of double entry bookkeeping (bookkeeping).

Luca Pachaulli is an Italian monk, professor and scholar. In 1494, in the second part "bookkeeping" of his monograph "summary of arithmetic, geometry, ratio and proportion", he systematically summarized the double entry bookkeeping popular in Venice, florence and other places in Italy at that time. It quickly spread all over Europe and all over the world, which not only caused the reform of accounting methods, but also marked the preliminary establishment of financial accounting theory.

1.6.4 Contemporary Accounting Stage

(1) Since the 1930s, the basic theory of accounting has been established.

(2) Accounting theories and methods have gradually been divided into two fields: In the 1950s, the separation of management accounting and financial accounting enriched the content of accounting and enhanced the function of accounting.

(3) Basic audit theory has been established: The basic theory of audit is a discipline formed by the accounting inspection based on the accounting, analysis and inspection of traditional financial accounting.

(4) Accounting computerization has emerged and been applied. Since the 1950s, applying scientific and technological achievements such as computers and the Internet in accounting has led to great changes in accounting methods.

(5) The advent of the era of intelligent finance has brought many changes to accounting.

Conclusion

Accounting is produced to meet the needs of the development of production activities, and develops and improves with the development of production. The more the economy develops, the more important accounting is. With the acceleration of the integration of global market economy, accounting, as the "world business language", will develop faster.

In this section we discuss about definition, function, procedure, elements and equations of accounting.

1.7 Def ine Accounting

What is accounting? We answered before: accounting is the language of economy (business), which helps us confirm, measure, record and report economic business tools. In China, there are two main views on what accounting is:

1.7.1 Accounting Information System Theory

Accounting information system theory holds that accounting is an information system, which is built to improve the economic benefits of enterprises and units and strengthen economic management. An economic information system mainly provides financial management information.

Basic functions of an accounting system: In developing information about the activities of a business, every accounting system performs the following basic functions:

(1) Interpret and record the effects of business transactions.

(2) Classify the effects of similar transactions in a manner that permits determination of the various totals and subtotals useful to management and used in accounting reports.

(3) Summarize and communicate the information contained in the system to decision-makers.

Accounting systems are designed to provide information that managers and outsiders can use in decision-making.

1.7.2 Management Activity Theory

Accounting is an important part of economic management. It is a management activity aimed at providing economic information and improving economic benefits. It takes money as the main unit of measurement and adopts a series of special procedures and methods to reflect and supervise the capital movement in the process of social reproduction.

It serves some purposes such as: to produce operating documents, to protect the company's assets, to provide data for company tax returns, and, in some cases, to provide the basis for reimbursement of costs by clients or customers. The accounting organization must also prepare documents that serve what might be called private information purposes.

Conclusion

(1) Language of business.

(2) The process by which businesses keep track of daily transactions and determine how the business is doing.

(3) Explain how efficiently and profitably resources invested in a business are being used.

1.8 Functions of Accounting

Basic functions of accounting in economic management (can be summarized as reflection function and supervision function).

1.8.1 Reflection (Accounting) Function of Accounting

According to the requirements of the accounting standards, the accountant shall use certain procedures and methods to comprehensively, systematically, timely and accurately calculate the economic business (transactions or events) of the accounting entity and provide information for the users of accounting information to make decisions.

1.8.2 Supervision (control) Function of Accounting

It refers to that the accountant controls the economic business (transaction or event) of the enterprise according to certain purposes and requirements, as well as relevant regulations and plans, to achieve the predetermined objectives.

Conclusion

The goal of a financial accounting report is to provide the users of financial accounting report with accounting information related to the financial status, operating results and cash flow of the enterprise, reflect the performance of the entrusted responsibilities of the enterprise management, and helped the users of financial accounting report makes economic decisions. Users of financial accounting reports include investors, creditors, the government and its relevant departments and the public.

1.9 Accounting Objectives

Accounting objective, also known as financial accounting reporting objective, refers to the purpose or final result that people intend to achieve through accounting under certain historical conditions.

Main Viewpoints of Financial Accounting Objectives of Modern Enterprises

(1) Decision usefulness: The goal of accounting is to provide information users (including investors, creditors and government departments) with useful information for their economic decision-making: including the financial status, operating results and other information of enterprises. The real information of enterprises, that is, emphasizing the usefulness (relevance) of information.

(2) Concept of fiduciary responsibility: The goal of accounting is that the entrusted party of resources (Enterprise Management) truthfully reflects the management and use of entrusted resources to the entrusting party of resources (investors, etc.) — historical and objective information of the enterprise, that is, emphasizing the reliability of information.

Conclusion

(1) Means of communicating business information.

(2) Provision of information to aid business decision-making.

(3) Means of establishing accountability.

(4) Provision of information to plan and control business activities.

(5) Provision of information to interested parties.

The goal a of financial accounting report is to provide the users of financial accounting reports with accounting information related to the financial status, operating results and cash flow of the enterprise, reflect the performance of the entrusted responsibilities of the enterprise management, and help the users of financial accounting report make economic decisions.

Users of financial accounting reports include investors, creditors, the government and its relevant departments and the public.

—Ministry of Finance: accounting standards for business enterprises — Basic Standards (2006).

1.10 Process of Accounting (Cycle of Accounting)

The accounting method during the process is as follows:

(1) Set up accounts.

(2) Double entry bookkeeping.

(3) Fill in and review vouchers.

(4) Register book.

(5) Cost calculation.

(6) Physical inventory.

(7) Preparation of financial and accounting reports.

1.10.1 Set up Accounts

According to the characteristics of the specific content of the accounting object and the requirements of economic management, the process of scientifically determining its classified items is a special method for classified accounting and supervising the accounting object.

The basic components of accounting objects are accounting elements, which will be learned in the following chapters.

1.10.2 Double Entry Bookkeeping

It is a special method for registering each economic business (transaction or event) in two or more relevant accounts with an equal amount. It must register each economic business in two or more interrelated accounts at the same amount, so that there is a corresponding relationship between two or more accounts involved in each economic business, and at the same time, the amounts recorded in the corresponding accounts are parallel and equal. Through the corresponding relationship of accounts, we can understand the content of economic business. Through the parallel relationship of accounts, you can check whether the records of relevant economic transactions are correct.

1.10.3 Fill in (or obtain) and Review Accounting Vouchers

Filling in and reviewing vouchers refers to a special method adopted to review whether economic business is reasonable and legal and ensure the correctness and completeness of account books and records. Accounting vouchers are written certificates that record economic transactions and clarify economic responsibilities. It is an important basis for registering account books. Whether the economic business is executed and completed depends on whether accounting vouchers have been obtained or filled in. Filling in and reviewing accounting vouchers can provide real and reliable accounting information for economic management.

1.10.4 Register Book

It is a special method to record the economic business in the account book according to the sequence of economic business. Account books are used for comprehensive, continuous and systematic records. The arrangement of various economic transactions is also an important tool for preserving accounting information. It has a certain structure and format, and should be registered according to the sequence of approved accounting vouchers. The various information provided by the account books is the main basis for preparing the accounting statements.

1.10.5 Cost Calculation

Cost calculation refers to a special method of collecting all expenses on a certain calculation object and recommending to determine the total cost and unit cost of each object. It usually refers to the cost calculation of manufacturing products. Cost calculation can assess and supervise whether various expenses incurred in the course of enterprise operation are saved so as to take measures to reduce costs and improve economic benefits. Cost calculation plays an important role in determining the scale of production compensation, correctly calculating and distributing national income, and formulating price policies.

1.10.6 Property Inventory

Property inventory is a special method to find out the actual amount of various assets, materials, receivables and monetary funds by checking the accounts through physical inventory, and to find out whether the actual amount is consistent with the amount in the accounts. Through property inventory, we can find out the custody and use of various assets, so as to take measures to tap the potential of materials and accelerate the turnover of funds. Property inventory plays an important role in ensuring the correctness of accounting data and supervising the safe and reasonable use of property.

1.10.7 Preparation of Financial Reports

Financial report refers to the document provided by an enterprise to reflect the financial status of an enterprise in a specific period, the operating results and cash flow of an accounting period. The preparation of financial reports is a summary of the daily accounting work. It is to regularly classify and summarize the contents of accounting records, form various indicators required by the users of accounting information, and then report them to the users of accounting information so that they can make decisions accordingly.

These seven aspects of accounting are interrelated and indispensable, forming a complete method system:

(1) Preset the account, select the bookkeeping method, and first obtain or fill in the accounting voucher after the transaction or event occurs.

(2) According to the accounting vouchers, double-entry bookkeeping method is adopted to register the account book (account).

(3) Carry out cost calculation and property inventory according to account books and records.

(4) At the end of the period, the financial report shall be prepared based on ensuring the consistency between accounts and facts.

From the perspective of accounting technology, the process of accounting can also include the following aspects:

(1) Analyzing: Analyzing is the first phase of the accounting process. The accountant must look at a transaction or event and determine its importance to the

business.

(2) Recording or Bookkeeping: Enter the information into the accounting system. It is the second phase. Traditionally this meant writing something by hand. Even today, much of the record keeping in accounting is done manually. However, some major changes in the business world have been caused by the introduction of computers. Even though the method of entering or recording accounting information has changed, the concept behind the process has not.

(3) Classifying: Group like transactions together. It is phase three of the process, relates to the grouping of like transactions together rather than keeping a narrative record of many transactions. Like items are grouped in separate accounts.

(4) Summarizing: Aggregate similar events to provide information that is easy to understand.

(5) Reporting: Reporting involves communicating results. In accounting, it is common to use tables of numbers rather than narrative-type reports. Sometimes, however, a combination of tables and narratives is used.

(6) Interpreting: The reported results is the final phase of the process. At this time, attention is directed to the significance of various matters and relationships. Percentage analyses and ratios are often used to help explain the difference among accounting periods. Foot-notes and special captions also may be valuable in the interpreting phase of accounting.

1.11 Accounting Elements

Accounting elements are the basic classification of accounting objects, the containerization of accounting objects, and the basic unit that reflects the financial status and operating results of accounting subjects.

China's "enterprise accounting standards—Basic Standards" strictly defines six accounting elements: assets, liabilities, owner's equity, income, expenses and profits. These six accounting elements can be divided into two categories, namely, accounting elements that reflect financial conditions (also known as balance sheet elements) and accounting elements that reflect operating results (also known as income statement elements). Among them, the accounting elements that reflect the financial situation include assets, liabilities and owner's equity, and the accounting elements that reflect the operating results include income, expenses and profits.

Next, we will elaborate on the specific content of each accounting element.

1.11.1 Assets

Assets refer to the resources formed by past transactions or events, owned or controlled by the enterprise and expected to bring economic benefits to the enterprise.

(1) Basic characteristics of asset elements:

① Past transactions or events of the enterprise: including the results of purchase, production or other transactions or events.

② The possible results of transactions or events expected to occur in the future do not belong to current assets.

③ Enterprise ownership or control: ownership refers to the ownership of a resource (such as equipment purchased by the enterprise); Control means that although the enterprise does not enjoy the ownership of a resource, the resource can be controlled by the enterprise (such as borrowing money, financing and leasing equipment).

④ Expected to bring economic benefits to the enterprise: it refers to the potential that directly or indirectly leads to the logistics of cash and cash equivalents into the enterprise-the most essential characteristics of asset elements. Resources without this feature can no longer be recognized as enterprise assets, such as houses and equipment that have been scrapped.

(2) Composition of asset elements:

Current assets refers to the assets that can be realized or consumed by an enterprise within one year or more than one business cycle (business cycle: the business period divided by the enterprise according to the characteristics of its business activities) .

It mainly includes cash on hand, bank deposits, receivables and prepayments, inventories, etc.

① Cash on hand refers to cash held by enterprises, which is called "cash" in traditional terms. Cash on hand is mainly used to pay small and sporadic expenses or expenditures incurred daily.

② Bank deposits refer to the funds deposited by enterprises in banks or other financial institutions. The bank or other financial institution is the "deposit bank" of the enterprise. The bank deposits of enterprises mainly come from the capital invested by investors, the funds from debt integration, and the payment for goods sold.

③ Receivables and prepayments refer to various claims incurred in the daily production and operation of an enterprise, including receivables (notes receivable, accounts receivable, other receivables, etc.) and prepayments.

④ Inventory refers to all kinds of materials or materials held for sale by an enterprise in the daily production and operation process, or still consumed in the production process, or consumed in the production or provision of labor services, including goods in stock, semi-finished products, products in process and various materials.

Non-current assets refer to assets that cannot be realized or consumed by an enterprise within one year or more than one business cycle.

① Long-term equity investment refers to the equity investment that has been held for more than one year (excluding one year) and cannot be realized or is not prepared to be realized or recovered within one year, including equity investments in subsidiaries and associated enterprises-the purpose is to obtain relatively stable investment income or control or influence the invested enterprise.

② Fixed assets refer to tangible assets with the following two characteristics at the same time: held for the production of goods, provision of labor services, lease or operation and management; The service life exceeds one accounting year, including houses, machinery and equipment, etc.

③ Intangible assets refer to identifiable non-monetary assets without physical form owned or controlled by the enterprise, including patent rights and trademark rights.

④ Investment real estate refers to the real estate held by an enterprise to earn rent or capital appreciation, or both.

⑤ Biological assets refer to the living animals and plants of the enterprise, such as livestock, crops and forests.

⑥ Other assets refer to various assets other than the above assets, such as long-term deferred expenses (such as preparation costs incurred during the establishment of the enterprise).

1.11.2 Liabilities

Liabilities refer to the current obligations formed by the past transactions and events of the enterprise and expected to cause economic benefits to flow out of the enterprise.

(1)Basic characteristics of debt elements:

① Current obligations arising from past transactions or events: It refers to the obligations undertaken by the enterprise under current conditions (such as signing loan contracts or receiving accounts payable bills in the past).

② It is expected to cause economic benefits to flow out of the enterprise: it refers to that cash and cash equivalents will flow out of the enterprise directly (such as paying off debts with monetary funds) or indirectly (such as paying off debts with physical assets) when performing realistic obligations (repaying debts).

③ It must be repaid with economic resources acceptable to creditors: in cash or cash equivalents; Promise new liabilities (issuing notes payable) to offset old debts, or the creditor will convert the liabilities owed by the enterprise into investment (owner's equity) in the enterprise.

(2)Composition of liabilities:

The liabilities of an enterprise can be divided into current liabilities (with a repayment period of no more than one year) and non-current liabilities (with a repayment period of more than one year).

Current liabilities refer to liabilities that the enterprise will repay within one year or more, including short-term borrowings, payables and advances.

① Short-term loans refer to all kinds of loans borrowed by enterprises from banks or other financial institutions with a term of less than one year, such as temporary loans obtained by enterprises from banks to supplement insufficient working capital.

② Accounts payable and advance receipts refer to various debts incurred by an enterprise in the daily production and operation process, mainly including accounts payable (notes payable, accounts payable, payroll payable, taxes payable, interest payable, dividends payable, other payables, etc.) and advance receipts.

Non-current liabilities refers to debts that the enterprise will repay in more than one year or more than one business cycle, including long-term loans, bonds payable and long-term accounts payable.

① Long-term loans refer to various loans borrowed by enterprises from banks or other financial institutions with a term of more than one year. Enterprises borrow long-term loans mainly to meet the capital needs of long-term projects.

② Bonds payable refer to long-term bonds actually issued by enterprises to raise long-term funds.

③ Long-term payables refer to other long-term payables other than long-term loans and bonds payable, including payables for imported equipment, payables for fixed assets under financing lease, etc.

1.11.3 Owner's Equity

Owner's equity refers to the residual equity enjoyed by the owner after deducting liabilities from the assets of the enterprise. It is the ownership of investors to the net assets of the enterprise.

(1) Basic characteristics:

① The owner refers to the provider of enterprise capital-investor, and in a joint-stock enterprise refers to the shareholder.

② Rights and interests: rights.

③ Residual equity: refers to the rights enjoyed by the owner after deducting liabilities from assets.

(2) Composition of owner's equity:

Owner's equity includes the capital invested by the owner (share capital), gains and losses directly included in the owner's equity, retained earnings, etc. It usually consists of paid-in capital (or share capital), capital reserve, surplus reserve and undistributed profits.

① Paid-in capital. The paid-in capital of an enterprise refers to the capital invested by the investor in the enterprise by the articles of association, contracts and agreements. It is one of the basic conditions for the registration and establishment of enterprises, and also the financial guarantee for enterprises to bear civil liability.

② Capital reserve. The capital reserve of an enterprise, also known as quasi capital, refers to the capital shared by the owners of the enterprise, which mainly comes from the premium and other capital reserves generated in the process of capital investment. The capital reserve is mainly used to increase capital.

③ Surplus reserve. Surplus reserves refer to retained earnings drawn from net profits by enterprises in accordance with laws and regulations. It includes:

④ Statutory surplus reserve, which refers to the surplus reserve withdrawn from the net profit by the enterprise in accordance with the proportion specified in the Company Law of the People's Republic of China (hereinafter referred to as the Company Law).

⑤ Discretionary surplus reserve, which refers to the surplus reserve withdrawn from the net profit by the enterprise in accordance with a certain proportion after the approval of the general meeting of shareholders or similar institutions. The surplus reserve of an enterprise can be used to make up for losses and to increase capital (or share capital). Enterprises that meet the prescribed conditions may also use surplus reserve to distribute cash dividends.

⑥ Undistributed profits. Undistributed profits refer to the profits reserved by the enterprise for future annual distribution. Undistributed profits and surplus reserves belong to retained earnings of the enterprise.

1.11.4 Income

Income refers to the total inflow of economic benefits formed in the daily activities of the enterprise, which will lead to the increase of owner's equity and have nothing to do with the capital invested by the owner.

(1)Basic characteristics of income factors:

① The inflow of economic benefits generated by the enterprise in its daily activities: the inflow of cash or cash equivalents for the enterprise.

② Income will eventually lead to the increase of owner's equity: it is determined by the relationship between income, expenses and profits and owner's equity.

③ It is strictly different from the profits generated from non daily activities (inventory profit of fixed assets, etc.).

④ The inflow of economic benefits that will not lead to the increase of owner's equity does not belong to income, such as advance payment from customers.

(2) Composition of income elements: It usually consists of main business income, other business income and investment income.

① Main business income: It refers to the income obtained from the daily main business of the enterprise (such as the income from the sales of automobiles by automobile manufacturing enterprises, the income from the sales of computers by computer manufacturing enterprises, etc.).

② Other business income: It refers to the income generated by other daily businesses of the enterprise (such as the income from the disposal of excess overstocked materials by product manufacturers, the income from the sales of auto parts by automobile manufacturers, the income from the sales of computer parts by computer manufacturers, etc.).

③ Investment income: It refers to the dividend and interest income obtained by enterprises from foreign investment (such as purchasing stocks and bonds of other enterprises).

It should be emphasized that the income mentioned above refers to income in a narrow sense, which is synonymous with business income. Income in a broad sense also includes gains directly included in current profits, namely non-operating income. Non-operating income refers to various incomes generated by an enterprise that are not directly related to its production and operation activities, including gains from scrapping non-current assets and donations.

④ Non-operating income: It refers to the occasional inflow of economic benefits in non-daily activities of the enterprise, such as the net income from the disposal of scrapped fixed assets, the fine income from the party fined, etc.

1.11.5 Expenses

Expenses refer to the total outflow of economic benefits incurred in the daily activities of the enterprise, which will lead to the reduction of owners' equity and have nothing to do with the distribution of profits to owners.

(1)Basic characteristics of expenses elements:

① The outflow of economic benefits generated by the enterprise in its daily activities: resulting in the logistics of cash or cash equivalents out of the enterprise. It is strictly different from the loss of non-daily activities, such as the net loss incurred by the enterprise in disposing damaged and scrapped fixed assets.

② Expenses will eventually lead to the reduction of owner's equity: it is determined by the relationship between expenses and income and profits. The outflow of economic benefits that will not reduce the owner's equity is not an expense, such as purchasing materials with deposits.

③ Expenses have nothing to do with the distribution of profits to owners: the distribution of profits to owners belongs to the distribution of operating results, not the outflow of economic benefits from daily activities of the enterprise.

(2)Composition of expense elements: It usually consists of main business cost, other business costs and investment loss, period expenses, etc.

① Main business cost. It refers to the cost incurred by the enterprise to obtain the main business income. For example, the cost of the automobile that the automobile manufacturer has sold is actually its production cost, etc.

② Other business costs. It refers to the cost incurred by the enterprise to obtain other business income. One example is the cost of overstocked parts sold by automobile manufacturing enterprises (in essence, it is their procurement cost), etc.

③ Taxes and surcharges. It refers to various taxes and fees paid by the enterprise in the process of operation, except value-added tax and income tax, such as consumption tax, urban construction tax and education surcharge.

④ Investment loss. It refers to the losses incurred by enterprises in foreign investment (such as purchasing stocks and bonds of other enterprises).

⑤ Period expenses. It refers to various expenses that cannot be included in the current operating cost, but should be directly included in the current profit and loss (including expenses and income, here refers to the expenses), such as sales expenses, administrative expenses and financial expenses.

⑥ Asset impairment loss. It refers to the loss caused by the impairment of the enterprise's asset value, such as bad debt loss of accounts receivable, impairment loss of fixed assets and inventory falling price loss.

⑦ Income tax expense. It refers to the tax payable to the tax authorities calculated and determined by the enterprise according to the realized profits in accordance with the provisions of the tax law.

The expenses defined above is also a narrow concept. In a broad sense, expenses also include losses directly included in current profits and income tax expenses. Losses directly included in the profits of the current period, namely non-operating expenditures, refer to various expenditures incurred by an enterprise that are not directly related to its production and operation activities, including inventory loss, net loss of scrapped fixed assets, net loss of scrapped intangible assets, loss of debt restructuring, public welfare donations and extraordinary losses.

⑧ Non-operating expenses. It refers to all kinds of expenses that occasionally occur in an enterprise and are not directly related to its daily activities, such as the inventory loss of fixed assets, the net loss of disposal of scrapped fixed assets and intangible assets, penalty expenses, donation expenses and extraordinary losses.

1.11.6 Profit

Profit refers to the operating results of an enterprise in a certain accounting period.

According to the content of profit, it is divided into operating profit, total profit and net profit. It includes the net amount of income minus expenses (operating profit), gains and losses directly included in the profits of the current period.

(1) Operating profit refers to the amount of main business income plus other business income minus main business costs, other business costs, taxes and surcharges, sales expenses, administrative expenses, financial expenses, asset impairment losses, plus investment income. It is the result of matching narrow income with narrow expense.

(2) Total profit refers to the amount of operating profit plus non-operating income minus non-operating expenses.

(3) Net profit, also known as after-tax profit, refers to the amount of total profits minus income tax expenses. It is the result of matching generalized income with generalized expense.

1.12 Accounting Equation

1.12.1 Meaning and Types of Accounting Equation

An accounting equation, also known as accounting identity, is an expression that uses mathematical balance to describe the quantitative relationship between the specific contents of accounting objects (i.e. accounting elements).

Types of accounting equations:

(1) static accounting equation.

(2) dynamic accounting equation.

(3) extended (integrated) accounting equation.

1.12.2 Static Accounting Equation (Basic Accounting Equation)

An equation composed of static accounting elements that indicate the financial position of an enterprise at a specific time date.

Combination method: Asset = Liability + Owner's Equity

Understanding of static accounting equations:

Firstly, the static accounting equation reflects two different aspects of the same fund: the existing form of the fund and the source channel of the fund.

Secondly, when measured in currency, the amounts of both sides of the accounting equation are equal.

Thirdly, assets will change in the same direction with the increase or decrease of liabilities and owner's equity. Assets will increase with the increase of liabilities and owner's equity, and will decrease with the decrease of liabilities and owner's equity, etc.

1.12.3 Dynamic Accounting Equation

An equation composed of dynamic accounting elements that reflects the operating results of an enterprise in a certain accounting period.

Combination method: Revenue - Expense = Profit

Understanding of dynamic accounting equations:

Firstly, the essence of profit is the difference between the realized income minus the relevant expenses. When the income exceeds the expense, it is a profit; When the income is less than the expense, it is a loss.

Secondly, profits will change in the same direction with the increase or decrease of income; profit increases with the increase of income; Profits decrease as revenue decreases.

Thirdly, profits will change in the opposite direction with the increase or decrease of expenses. (Profits decrease with the increase of expenses, and increase with the decrease of expenses).

1.12.4 Extended (Integrated) Accounting Equation

An equation that comprehensively reflects the financial status and operating results of an enterprise, which is a combination of static and dynamic accounting equations.

Combination mode: Assets + Expenses = Liabilities + Owner's Equity + Income

Understanding of extended accounting equation:

Firstly, the expansion of funds in two different aspects: the existence form of funds and the source channel of funds.

Secondly, both sides of the equation are new equality based on the increase of quantity.

Assets = Liabilities + Owner's Equity + Profits
= Liabilities + Owner's Equity + (Revenue-Expenses)
Assets + Expenses = Liabilities + Owner's Equity + Income

The above analysis shows that there is an identity relationship between the six accounting elements of assets, liabilities, owner's equity, income, expenses and profits. The accounting equation reflects this identity relationship, so it is always true. The occurrence of any economic business cannot break the balance of the accounting equation.

1.12.5 The Effects of Transaction on the Accounting Equation

Any activity of a business which affects the accounting equation is a transaction. Transactions are recorded in the accounting records using the cost principle. The actual amount paid or received is the amount recorded. Buying and selling assets, performing service and borrowing money are common business transactions.

(1) The basic accounting equation: assets = liabilities + owner's equity. The effect of any transaction on the accounting equation may be indicated by increasing or decreasing a special asset, liability or owner's equity element. To illustrate, assume the following transactions took place during January, 2022, for ABC company. The effect of these transactions on the accounting equation can be analyzed as follows:

Transaction 1: The owner invested $100 000 cash in the business.

Effect on Accounting Equation: An increase in an asset offset by an increase in owner's equity.

Analysis: This transaction increased the asset Cash. Since the owner contributed the asset, the owner's equity—Capital—is increased by the same amount. The equation for the business would appear as follows:

Assets	=	Liabilities	+ Owner's Equity
Cash			Capital
(1) +$100 000			+$100 000
$100 000	=		$100 000

Total Assets: 100 000 = Liabilities + Owner's Equity 100 000.

Transaction 2: purchased office equipment on credit with the invoice amount $5 000.

Effect on Accounting Equation: An increase in an asset offset by an increase in a liability.

Analysis: The company purchased office equipment (desks, chairs, file cabinet, etc.) for $5 000 on credit.This transaction caused the asset Office Equipment to increase by $5 000. The liability Account Payable increased by the same amount. There was no effect on the owner's equity. The accounting equation now looks like this:

Assets		= Liabilities	+ Owner's Equity
Cash +	Office Equip.	Accounts Payable	Capital
(2) $100 000	+$5 000	+$5 000	$100 000
$100 000 +	$5 000 =	$5 000	+$100 000

Total Assets: 105 000 = Liabilities 5 000 + Owner's Equity 100 000.

Transaction 3: purchased office supplies for cash, $1 000.

Effect on Accounting Equation: An increase in one asset offset by a decrease in another asset.

Analysis: The company purchased office supplies (stationery, legal pads, pencils, etc.) for cash, $1 000. This transaction caused a $1 000 decrease in the asset Cash. The asset Office Supplies increased by $1 000. The effect on the equation is as follows:

Assets			=Liabilities	+ Owner's Equity
Cash +	Office Supp.	Office Equip.	Accounts Payable	Capital
$100 000		$5 000	$5 000	$100 000
(3) −1 000	+ 1 000			
$99 000 +	$1 000	+ $5 000 =	$5 000	+$100 000

Total Assets: 105 000 = Liabilities 5 000 + Owner's Equity100 000.

Transaction 4: paid amount owed to a creditor, $1 000.

Effect on Accounting Equation: A decrease in an asset offset by a decrease in a liability.

Analysis: The company paid $1 000 on account to the company from which the office equipment purchased. Earlier, the company purchased office equipment on credit. The office equipment account increased and the liability Accounts Payable increased. Now the company is going to make a payment on this account. This payment caused both the asset Cash and the liability Accounts Payable to decrease by $1 000. The effect on the equation is as follows:

Assets			= Liabilities +	Owner's Equity
Cash +	Office Supp.	Office Equip.	Accounts Payable	Capital
$99 000	$1 000	$5 000	$5 000	$100 000
(4)-1 000			-1 000	
$98 000 +	$1 000	+ $5 000	$4 000 +	$100 000

Total Assets: 104 000 = Liabilities 4 000 + Owner's Equity 100 000.

Transaction 5: purchased office supplies on credit, $4 000.

Effect on Accounting Equation: An increase in an asset offset by an increase in a liability.

Analysis: The company purchased office supplies on account for $4 000. This transaction caused the asset Office Supplies to increase by $4 000 and increase the liability Account Payable by the same amount. The effect of this transaction on the equation is as follows:

Assets			= Liabilities +	Owner's Equity
Cash	+ Office Supp.	+ Office Equip.	Accounts Payable	Capital
(5) $98 000	$1 000	$5 000	$4 000	$100 000
	+ $4 000		+ $4 000	
$98 000	+ $5 000	+ $5 000	= $8 000 +	$100 000

Total Assets: 108 000 = Liabilities 8 000 + Owner's Equity 100 000.

(2) Dynamic accounting equation: Revenues − Expenses = Profits

Transaction 6: received cash as payment for professional fees, $3 500.

Effect on Accounting Equation: An increase in an asset offset by an increase in owner's equity.

Analysis: The company received $3 500 cash from a client for professional services performed. This transaction caused the asset Cash to increase by $3 500.

Since cash was received for services performed, owner's equity also increased. Professional Fees is the account title used for revenue. The effect of this transaction on the equation is as follows:

Assets			= Liabilities +	Owner's Equity	
Cash	+ Office Supp.	+ Office Equip.	Accounts Payable	Capital −Expense	+Revenue
$98 000	$5 000	$5 000	$8 000	$100 000	
(6) +$3 500					+$3 500
$101 500	+ $5 000	+ $5 000	= $8 000 +	$100 000	+$3 500

Total Assets: 111 500 = Liabilities 8 000 + Owner's Equity 103 500.

Transaction 7: paid office rent of $1 000.

Effect on Accounting Equation: A decrease in an asset offset by a decrease in owner's equity.

Analysis: The company paid $1 000 for office rent for January. This transaction caused the asset Cash to decrease by $1 000, with an equal reduction in owner's equity. Owner's equity was decreased because of rent expense. The effect of this transaction on the equation is as follows:

Assets			= Liabilities +	Owner's Equity		
Cash	+ Office Supp.	+ Office Equip.	Accounts Payable	Capital	−Expense	+Revenue
$101 500	$5 000	$5 000	$8 000	$100 000		$3 500
(7) −$1 000					− $1 000	
$100 500	+ $5 000	+ $5 000	= $8 000 +	$100 000	− $1 000	+ $3 500

Total Assets: 110 500 = Liabilities 8 000 + Owner's Equity 102 500.

Transaction 8: paid telephone expense, $750.

Effect on Accounting Equation: A decrease in an asset offset by a decrease in owner's equity.

Analysis: The company paid a bill for telephone service, $750.This transaction, like the previous one, decreased the asset Cash, and also decreased owner's equity.

Owner's equity was decreased because of the Telephone Expense. The effect of this transaction on the equation is as follows:

Assets			= Liabilities +	Owner's Equity		
Cash	+ Office Supp.	+ Office Equip.	Accounts Payable	Capital	−Expense	+Revenue
$100 500	$5 000	$5 000	$8 000	$100 000	$1 000	$3 500
(8) −$750					− $750	
$99 750	+ $5 000	+ $5 000	= $8 000 +	$100 000	− $1 750	+ $3 500

Total Assets: 109 750 = Liabilities 8 000 + Owner's Equity 101 750.

From the above analysis, we know that every business transaction, no matter how simple or how complex, can be expressed in terms of its effect on the accounting equation. Each business transaction makes at least two effects on the accounting equation that always keeps balance after every business transaction was finished, i.e., the total amount of left side equals to that of the right side.

Chapter 2　Accounting Concepts and Standards

Learning Objectives:

(1) Understand fundamental accounting assumptions.

(2) Understand qualitative characteristics of accounting information.

(3) Understand the recognition and measurement requirements of accounting elements.

2.1 Fundamental Accounting Assumptions

Accounting assumptions, also known as the basic premise of accounting, refer to the reasonable setting of the spatial scope, time scope, basic procedures and measurement methods of accounting in order to ensure the normal progress of accounting work and the quality of accounting information.

2.1.1 Contents of Accounting Assumptions

(1) Accounting entity assumption.

(2) Going concern assumption.

(3) Accounting period assumption.

(4) Monetary unit assumption.

2.1.2 Accounting Entity Assumption

An enterprise shall recognize, measure and report its own transactions or events in specific units or organizations served by accounting.

Under this concept, for accounting purposes, all kinds of business concerns are conceived and treated as a separate entity, separate and distinct from its owners and from other concerns. Either the transactions or the assets of a concern should not include those of the owner or owners. As for the transactions between the concern and the owners in accounting procedures, they should be treated as those with other concerns. As a result, all the accounting records and reports should be made by a concern as an independent entity rather than by owners personally.

Significance of accounting entity assumption:

(1) Clarify the space scope of accounting work, and solve the problem of accounting for whose economic business and bookkeeping for whom.

(2) The assumption of accounting entity is the basis of going concern, accounting installment and monetary measurement assumptions, as well as another accounting basis.

2.1.3 Going Concern Assumption

The accounting recognition, measurement and reporting of an enterprise shall be based on continuous operation.

Most accounting methods are based on the assumption that the business enterprise will have a long life. Experience indicates that, in spite of numerous business failures, companies have a fairly high continuance rate. Although accountants do not believe that business firms will last indefinitely, they do expect them to last long enough to fulfill their objectives and commitments.

The going-concern concept, which holds that the entity will remain in operation for the foreseeable future. Most assets—that is, the firm's resources, such as office supplies, lands, buildings, and equipment—are acquired for use rather than for sale. Under the going concern concept,accountants assume that the business will remain in operation long enough to use existing assets for their intended purpose. The market value of an asset or the price at which the asset can be sold—may change during the asset's life. Moreover, historical cost is a more reliable accounting measure for assets than market value because cost is a historical fact.

A balance sheet is prepared under the assumption that the concern for which the statement is made will continue in operation, so far a going concern's assets used in carrying on its operations are not for sale. Their current market values are not relevant and need not be shown. Also, without a sale, their current market values usually cannot be objectively established as is required by the "objectivity principle".

Significance of going concern assumption:

(1) Clarify the time range of accounting work—transactions or events that occurred during the normal operation of the enterprise.

(2) It is the basis of a reasonable selection of accounting procedures and methods, such as amortization of intertemporal expenses, provision for depreciation of fixed assets, etc.

(3) It is the basis of the assumption of "accounting installment".

2.1.4 Accounting Period Assumption

An enterprise shall divide accounting periods, settle accounts by stages and prepare financial and accounting reports. The continuous operation process is artificially divided into several periods for the purpose of timely accounting reports.

Life of a business often lasts many years and its activities go on without interruption over the years. However, the most accurate way to measure the results of enterprise activities would be to measure them at the time of the enterprise's eventual liquidation. Business, government, investors, and various other user groups, however, cannot wait indefinitely for such information. Accountants must provide financial information periodically, so that all users make their decisions upon the information.

The accounting period or time period assumption simply implies that the economic activities of an enterprise can be divided into artificial time periods of equal length. These time periods vary, but the most common are monthly, quarterly, and yearly.

Significance of accounting installment assumption:

(1) Clarify the basic procedures of accounting, and clarify the time of bookkeeping, accounting and reimbursement.

(2) It defines the concepts of the current period, early period and later period, which can accurately provide the data of financial status and operating results of each period, and also facilitate the comparison of accounting information of each period.

2.1.5 Monetary Measurement Assumptions

The accounting of an enterprise shall be measured in currency. Take currency as the main measurement unit to record and report the operation of the enterprise (supplemented by physical quantity, labor hours and other measurement units).

Accounting is based on the assumption that money is the common denominator by which economic activity is conducted, and that the monetary unit provides an appropriate basis for accounting measurement and analysis. This assumption implies that the monetary unit is the most effective means of expressing to interested parties changes in capital and exchanges of goods and services. The monetary unit is relevant, simple, universally available, understandable, and useful. Application of this assumption is dependent on the even more basic assumption that quantitative data are useful in communicating economic information and in making rational economic decisions.

In the United States, accountants record transactions in dollars because the dollar is the medium of exchange. British accountants record transactions in pounds sterling, and Japanese accountants in yen.

Unlike the value of a liter or a mile, the value of a dollar or of a Mexican peso changes over time. A rise in the general price level is called inflation. During inflation, a dollar will purchase less milk, less toothpaste, and less of other goods. When prices are stable—when there is little inflation—a dollar's purchasing power is also stable.

Accountants assume that the dollar's purchasing power is relatively stable. The stable monetary unit concept is the basis for ignoring the effect of inflation in the accounting records. It allows accountants to add and subtract dollar amounts as though each dollar has the same purchasing power as any other dollar at any other time.

Significance of monetary measurement assumptions:

(1) Clarify the measurement method of accounting. Money is the general equivalent of commodities, which can be used to measure all accounting elements and facilitate synthesis and comparison.

(2) It can overcome the differences of physical measurement units and the complexity of labor measurement units, and obtain comprehensive value indicators.

(3) The value indicators measured in monetary units have the advantages of comprehensiveness and comparability, and are widely used in practice.

2.2 Qualitative Characteristics of Accounting Information

As a management activity, one of the main purposes of accounting is to provide the stakeholders of enterprises with accounting information that reflects the entrusted responsibilities of operators and provides investors with decision-making. To achieve this goal, accounting information must have certain quality characteristics. Accounting information quality characteristics are also called accounting information quality requirements and accounting information quality standards. According to the Accounting Standards for Business Enterprises—Basic Standards, the quality characteristics of accounting information include the following eight items: reliability, relevance, understandability, comparability, substance over form, importance, prudence and timeliness. These quality characteristics require accountants to follow these quality requirements for accounting information when dealing with accounting business and providing accounting information, so as to better serve the stakeholders of the enterprise.

The quality characteristics of accounting information are the basic requirements for the quality of accounting information provided in enterprise financial reports and the basic characteristics of accounting information.

2.2.1 Reliability (Objectivity and Authenticity)

An enterprise shall conduct accounting recognition, measurement and reporting based on actual transactions or events, truthfully reflect various accounting elements and other relevant information that meet the recognition and measurement requirements, and ensure the authenticity, reliability and integrity of accounting information. It must truthfully reflect the financial situation, operating results and cash flow of the enterprise, and ensure that the content is true, the figures are accurate and the data are reliable. Accounting personnel shall maintain an objective and fair position in handling.

2.2.2 Relevance (Usefulness)

The accounting information provided by the enterprise shall be related to the economic decision-making needs of the users of the financial accounting report, and help the users of the financial accounting report to evaluate or predict the past, present or future situation of the enterprise. In the process of confirming, measuring and reporting accounting information, enterprises should fully consider the decision-making mode and information needs of users. Accounting information should be as relevant as possible on the premise of reliability, so as to meet the decision-making needs of investors and other users of financial reports.

2.2.3 Understandability (Clarity)

The information provided by the enterprise shall be clear and easy for the users of financial and accounting reports to understand and use. The accounting records shall be accurate and clear, and the accounting books filled in accounting vouchers and registered must have legal basis, clear account correspondence and complete text summary. In the preparation of accounting statements, the project articulation relationship is clear, the content is complete and the figures are accurate.

2.2.4 Comparability

The accounting information provided by an enterprise shall be comparable. For the same or similar transactions or events occurring in different periods, consistent accounting policies shall be adopted and shall not be changed at will. For the same or similar transactions or events that occurred in different enterprises, the prescribed accounting policies shall be adopted to ensure the consistency and comparability of accounting information.

2.2.5 Substance over Form

An enterprise shall carry out accounting recognition, measurement and reporting in accordance with the economic essence of the transaction or event, and shall not only take the legal form of the transaction or event as the basis. An enterprise shall conduct accounting recognition, measurement and reporting in accordance with the economic essence of the transaction or event, not just based on the legal form of the transaction or event.

2.2.6 Materiality

The accounting information provided by an enterprise shall reflects all important transactions or events related to the financial position, operating results and cash flow of the enterprise. Important economic businesses shall be accounted for separately and reflected by items, strive to be accurate, and make key explanations in the financial report. For unimportant economic business, without affecting the authenticity of accounting information, accounting can be appropriately simplified or consolidated, so as to focus on the key.

2.2.7 Prudence (Conservatism)

An enterprise shall be cautious in accounting recognition, measurement and reporting of transactions or events, and shall not overestimate assets or income, or underestimate liabilities or expenses. It is helpful for enterprises to make correct business decisions. And it is conducive to protecting the interests of investors and creditors, to improving the competitiveness of enterprises in the market.

2.2.8 Timeliness

An enterprise shall make timely accounting recognition, measurement and report on the transactions or events that have occurred, and shall not mention them in advance or with delay. It can help to collect accounting information in time, handle accounting information in time and timely transfer accounting information.

2.3 Understand the Recognition and Measurement Requirements of Accounting Elements

The recognition and measurement of accounting elements should not only meet certain conditions, but also follow the following requirements in the process of recognition and measurement, including historical cost concepts, matching principle, distinguishing revenue expenditure and capital expenditure, etc. So the section will be illustrated as follows:

(1) Historical cost concepts.

(2) Matching principle.

(3) Capital and revenue expenditure.

(4) Accrual basis and cash basis.

2.3.1 Historical Cost Concepts

Historical cost measurement, also known as actual cost measurement or original cost measurement, refers to that all properties and materials of an enterprise shall be valued according to the actual expenses incurred at the time of acquisition or purchase and construction.When prices change, unless otherwise stipulated by the state, the book value shall not be adjusted.

Traditionally, users of financial statements have found that cost is generally the most useful basis for accounting measurement and reporting. Under the cost principle, all goods and services purchased by an enterprise are recorded at acquisition cost and appear on financial statement at cost. This is often referred to as the historical cost principle.

The cost principle states that acquired assets and services should be recorded at their actual cost (also called historical cost). Even though the purchaser may believe the price paid is a bargain, the item is recorded at the price paid in the transaction and not at the "expected" cost. Suppose your stereo shop purchases stereo equipment from a supplier who is going out of business. Assume that you get a good deal on this purchase and pay only $4 000 for merchandise that would have cost you $3 000 elsewhere. The cost principle requires you to record this merchandise at its actual cost of $4 000, not the $3 000 that you believe it is worth.

The cost principle also holds that accounting records should maintain the historical cost of an asset for as long as the business holds the asset. Why? Because cost is a reliable measure. Suppose your store holds the stereo equipment for six months. During that time, stereo prices increase and the equipment can be sold for $3 500. Should its accounting value—the figure "on the books" —be the actual cost of $4 000 or the current market value of $3 500? According to the cost principle, the accounting value of the equipment remains at actual cost, $4 000.

2.3.2 Matching Principle

Matching principle requires that revenues and expenses be matched. It is well recognized that a business incurs expenses in order to earn revenues. The revenues earned are the results of the expenses paid. Consequently it is only proper that expenses should be matched with the revenues they helped to produce.

In recognizing expenses, accountants attempt to follow the approach of "let the expense follow the revenue". Expenses are recognized not when wages are paid, or when the work is performed, or when a product is produced, but when the work (service) or the product actually makes its contribution to revenue. Thus, expense recognition is tied to revenue recognition. This practice is referred to as the matching principle because it dictates that efforts (expenses) should be matched with the revenues whenever it is reasonable and practicable to do so.

In conclusion, the matching of income and expense includes two aspects: one is the matching of income and expense in the causal relationship, that is, certain expenditures occur when a certain amount of income is obtained, and the purpose of these expenditures is to obtain these revenues; The second is the matching of income and expense in the sense of time, that is, the matching of income and expense in a certain accounting period.

2.3.3 Revenue Expenditure and Capital Expenditure

The accounting entity shall reasonably divide the revenue expenditure and capital expenditure. Where the benefit of the expenditure is only related to the current accounting year (or one business cycle), it shall be regarded as a revenue expenditure. Where the benefit of the expenditure is related to several accounting years (or above one business cycle), it shall be regarded as a capital expenditure.

Revenue expenditure is the expenditure incurred to obtain the income of the current period which shall be included in the current profit and loss as the expense of the current period and included in the income statement, such as the cost of goods sold, period expenses, income tax, etc. If revenue expenditure is treated as capital expenditure, it will result in less expenses and more assets. If a capital expenditure is treated as revenue expenditure, it will result in a false increase in current profits and a higher asset value.

Capital expenditure is various ans is incurred to form production and operation capacity and obtain income in subsequent periods which shall be included in the balance sheet as assets, such as expenditures for the purchase of fixed assets and intangible assets. If a capital expenditure is treated as revenue expenditure, it will result in more expenses and fewer assets, and a false decrease in current profits and a lower asset value. The purpose of dividing income expenditure and capital expenditure is to correctly determine the current profit and loss of an enterprise (generally an accounting year). The following table shows the financial statement effect of the deferential treatment.

Exhibit 2-1　The Financial Statement Effect of the Deferential Treatment

Treatment	Financial Statement Effect			
	Statement	Expense	Current Profit	Current Taxes
Capital Expenditure	Statement of financial position account debited	Deferred	Higher	Higher
Revenue Expenditure	Income statement account debited	Currently recognized	Lower	Lower

Example 2.1: DHP Autos has spent the following amounts in the last financial year relating to the purchase and operation of a pick-up truck.

	£
Cost of purchasing pick-up truck	12 000
Painting business logo on side of van	400
Replacing worn-out tyres	360
Road tax for year	150
Fuel costs for year	980
Upgrading of truck with new engine	2 400

The expenditure can be classified into capital and revenue expenditure as shown in Exhibit 2-2.

Exhibit 2-2 The Classification of Expenditure Into Capital and Revenue Expenditure

Example	Type of expenditure	Explanation	Capital expenditure	Revenue expenditure
Cost of purchasing pick-up truck	Capital	Buying new asset	£12 000	
Painting business logo on side of van	Capital	Adding value to asset	£400	
Replacing worn-out tyres	Revenue	Not adding value, day-to-day running expense		£360
Road tax for year	Revenue	Regular expense incurred every year		£150
Fuel costs for year	Revenue	Regular, day-to-day expense		£980
Upgrading of truck with new engine	Capital	One-off expense- adding value to asset	£2 400	
Totals			£14 800	£1 490

2.3.4 Accrual Basis and Cash Basis

Accrual basis and cash basis are two basic methods to recognize transactions or events (especially those related to income and expenses). In the process of transaction, the period of income and expenditure related to revenue and expenses is often inconsistent with its attribution period. In order to ensure the reasonable matching of relevant revenue and relevant expenses, we should study the method (basis) for recognition.

The accrual basis, also known as the accrual basis and the A/R and A/P basis, is a method to recognize the revenue and expenses of the current period based on the "A/R and A/P" standard. When the accrual basis is adopted, all revenues realized in the current period and expenses incurred or borne in the current period, regardless of whether the funds are received or paid, shall be treated as income and expenses of the current period; All revenues and expenses that do not belong to the current period cannot be treated as revenues and expenses of the current period even if the funds have been received and paid in the current period.

In accrual-basis accounting, an accountant recognizes the impact of a business trans action as it occurs. When the business performs a service, makes a sale, or incurs an expense, the accountant must enter the transaction into the journals, whether cash has been received or paid or not. Most businesses use the accrual-basis.

Under the accrual basis, revenues are reported in the income statement in the period in which they are earned. For example, revenue is reported when the services are provided to customers. Cash may or may not be received from customers during this period. The concept that supports this reporting of revenues is called the revenue recognition concept.

Accrual-basis accounting can provide more complete information than cash-basis accounting does, which is very important for decision-makers.

Accrual-basis accounting is more complex—and more complete—than cash-basis. Accrual-basis accounting records cash transactions, including:

(1) Collecting from customers.

(2) Receiving cash from interest earned.

(3) Paying salaries, rent, income tax, and other expenses.

(4) Borrowing money.

(5) Paying off loans.

(6) Issuing stock.

It also records such non-cash transactions as:

(1) Purchases of inventory on credit.

(2) Sales on credit.

(3) Accrual of interest and other expenses incurred but not yet paid.

(4) Depreciation expense.

(5) Usage of prepaid insurance, supplies, and other prepaid expenses.

The accrual-basis accounting is designed to avoid misleading income statement results that could otherwise result from the timing of cash receipts and payments. If the income statement is to portray a realistic net income figure based upon accrual accounting, all revenues earned during the period and all expenses incurred must be shown. Therefore, it is often necessary to adjust some account balances at the end of each accounting period to achieve a proper matching of costs and expenses with revenue. The adjusting step occurs after the journals have been posted, but before financial statements are prepared.

Characteristics of revenues and expenses recognized on accrual basis:

(1) Consider advances and prepayments, as well as accrued income and accrued expenses.

(2) The daily account books and records cannot fully reflect the revenues and expenses of the current period, and the account items shall be adjusted at the end of the accounting period.

(3) The accounting procedures are complex, which reflect the revenues and expenses in different accounting periods, and can correctly calculate the operating results.

(4) Scope of application: manufacturing enterprises, etc.

Cash basis: cash basis, also known as cash basis or paid-in cash basis, is a method to determine the current revenues and expenses based on the "actual receipt and payment of funds". The key point is that all payments received in the current period, whether or not attributable to the current period, are treated as current income; All payments made in the current period, whether or not attributable to the current period, are treated as current expenses.

In cash-basis accounting, the accountant records a transaction only when cash is received or paid. Cash receipts are treated as revenues and payments are handled as expenses. It ignores receivables, payables, and depreciation. Only very small businesses use the cash-basis.

Under the cash basis, revenues and expenses are reported in the income statement in the period in which cash is received or paid. For example, fees are recorded when cash is received from clients, and wages are recorded when cash is paid to employees. The net income (or net loss) is the difference between the cash receipts (revenues) and the cash payments (expenses).

The cash basis does not emphasize the matching principle. Instead, the receipt or payment of cash governs the recording process. Thus, the income statement under the cash basis could provide an unrealistic picture of the company's operations.

Characteristics of revenue and expenses recognized on cash basis:

(1) Advances and prepayments, as well as accrued revenues and accrued expenses are not considered. As long as the payment has been received or paid, it will be treated as current revenues and expenses.

(2) At the end of the accounting period, the income and expenses of the current period are determined according to the account books and records, and there is no problem of closing account adjustment.

(3) The accounting procedures are simple, emphasizing the practicability of financial status, but lacking the comparability of different accounting periods.

(4) Scope of application: administrative and public institutions.

To further illustrate the problem, here examples to compare the two accounting treatment bases in the Exhibit 2-3.

Exhibit 2-3 Comparison between the accrual basis and cash basis

	Example	Accrual basis	Cash basis
1	The rent of the leased house in the first half of the year is received once in January	The rent income in January is 1/6 of the total income; The rest of the revenue in January is the revenue collected in advance	All is the revenue in January
2	In January, the rent of office equipment for the next two years, including this month, will be paid at a time	The rent in January is only 1/24 of the total expenditure; The rest is regarded as prepaid expenses in January	All of them are regarded as expenses in January
3	Sign a contract with the buyer in the three batches of products which were sold in Jan/Feb/Mar, and the payment for goods was settled at the end of March	As the income of January, February and March respectively; The income earned but not received in January and February is the accrued income	All are taken as the income in March
4	Borrow a three-month loan from the bank in January, and repay the interest once it is due (i.e. in March)	As the expenses of January, February and March respectively; Expenses incurred but unpaid in January and February are accrued expenses	All as expenses in March
5	The amount received in the current period is the income that should be obtained in the current period, and the amount paid in the current period is the expense that should be borne in the current period, so the results of recognizing income and expense on the accrual basis and the cash basis are identical		

Chapter 3   The Double-Entry System of Accounting

Learning Objectives:

(1) Understand the format of accounts.

(2) Understand the chart of accounts.

(3) Understand how to design accounts.

(4) Understand how to use the double-entry system.

In order to conduct accounting practice and exercise accounting supervision, accounting personnel need some basic accounting skills. These skills include how to classify accounting elements and establish the accounting equation, how to design accounts with the double-entry system, and how to conduct accounting practice concerning transactions and costs incurred in a company's operation. In detail, accounting elements are made up of assets, liabilities, owner's equity, revenue, expenses and profits. Among them equations exist, so accounting equations express their relationships. Accounting elements are named accounting titles (the chart of accounts) which are also the names of accounts. Accounts record the changes of accounting elements with debit and credit bookkeeping as a common tool.

3.1 Accounts and Format of Accounts

3.1.1 Accounts

As we earliev mentioned, business transactions were recorded and summarized in the accounting equation format. However, this format is difficult to use when thousands of transactions must be recorded daily. Thus accounting systems are designed to show the increases and decreases in each financial statement item in a separate record. This record is called an account.

The assets of a business may consist of a number of items, such as cash and office supplies. A form or record used to keep track of the increases and decreases in each item is known as an account. Accounts are used to maintain an orderly record of all transactions affecting that item. The following accounts (Figure 3-1) with their account classification are used in the example of Peter Jonathan, a dentist:

Assets	Liabilities	Owner's Equity
Cash	Short-term Loans	Peter Jonathan, Capital
Accounts Receivable	Accounts Payable	Peter Jonathan, Drawing
Office Equipment		
Revenue	Expenses	
Professional Fees	Rent Expense	
	Salaries Expense	

Figure 3-1 Account Example of Peter Jonathan

3.1.2 Format of Accounts

(1) The T-accounts: To record transactions, accountants often use T-accounts, which is the simplest form of an account. A T-account is commonly used for instructional purposes. It consists of a two-line drawing resembling the capital letter

T. The term gets its name from that. The vertical line divides the account into its two sides: left and right. The Account title rests on the horizontal line at the top of the T. Therefore, the T-account has three parts: a title, which is the name of the account; a space for recording increases in the amount of the item; a space for recording decreases in the amount of the item.

Transactions are entered in T-accounts as follows:

- Increases in an account are entered on one side of the T, and decreases are entered on the other side.
- The account balance is determined by subtracting the total decreases from the total increases.

Figure 3-2 shows a general example of T-account.

Cash (Title)

Debit	Credit
(Left side)	(Right side)

Figure 3-2　T-Account Format

(2) Four-column account format: The ledger accounts illustrated thus far have been in a two-column T-account format, with the debit column on the left and the credit column on the right. The T-account clearly distinguishes debits from credits and is often used for illustrative purposes that do not require much detail.

Another standard format has four amount columns, as illustrated for the Cash account in Exhibit 3-1. The first pair of amount columns is for the debit and credit amounts posted from journal entries. The second pair of amount columns is for the account's balance. This four-column format keeps a running balance in the two rightmost columns of the account. For this reason, the four-column format is used more often than the two-column format. In Exhibit 3-1, Cash has a debit balance of $50 000 after Air & Sea's first transaction and a debit balance of $10 000 after its second transaction is posted. The "J. 1" in the Journal Reference column indicates that the posted amount comes from journal page 1.

Exhibit 3-1 Four-column Account Format

Account: Cash						Account No. 111
Date	Item	Post. Ref.	Debit	Credit	Balance	
					Debit	Credit
2022						
Apr. 1		J. 1	$50 000		$50 000	
		J. 1		$40 000	$10 000	

The account you see is called a four-column account. It is different from the T-account, but it accomplishes the same purpose. In the T-account, you added the left side (debits) and then the right side (credits) to see which was larger. Then you subtracted the smaller from the larger, and the balance remaining was on the side with the larger amount. In the four-column account, you first enter the amount and then compute a new balance. After each entry is posted, the new account balance is computed.

(3) Normal balance of an account: An account's normal balance is on the side of the account—debit or credit—where increases are recorded. That is, the normal balance is on the side that is positive. For example, because cash and other assets usually have a debit balance (the debit side is positive and the credit side negative), the normal balance of assets is on the debit side. Assets are called debit-balance accounts. Conversely, because liabilities and stockholders' equity usually have a credit balance, their normal balances are on the credit side. They are called credit-balance accounts. Exhibit 3-2 illustrates the normal balance of all the assets, liabilities, and stockholders' equities, including revenues and expenses.

An account that normally has a debit balance may occasionally have a credit balance, which indicates a negative amount of the item. For example, Cash will have a temporary credit balance if the entity overdraws its bank account. Similarly, liability Accounts Payable—normally a credit-balance account—will have a debit balance if the entity overpays its account. In other instances, the shift of a balance amount away from its normal balance indicates an accounting error. For example, a credit balance in Office Supplies, Office Furniture, or Buildings indicates an error because negative amounts of these assets do not exist.

Exhibit 3-2 Normal Balances of Accounts

Assets	Debit	
Liabilities		Credit
Stockholders' equity		Credit
Common stock		Credit
Retained earnings		Credit
Dividends	Debit	
Revenues		Credit
Expense	Debit	

Adding a separate account means writing its corresponding account title on the page(s) of an account book. The numerous accounts in the account book are called ledger accounts. There are two types of ledgers in ordinary use: general ledgers and subsidiary (or specific) ledgers. An account usually shows four kinds of amounts in a specific accounting period, namely the beginning balance, increase sum, decrease sum and ending balance. The relationship among them is shown below:

Ending Balance=Beginning Balance + Increase Sum-Decrease Sum

(4) The chart of accounts: Prior to journalizing, the bookkeeper must know which account to use, or which account to debit and which to credit. One of the first things a new business does is to determine what accounts it will use in its day-to-day operations. In China, there are six groups of account titles such as assets, liabilities, common subjects, owner's equity, costs, and profits and losses. The chart of accounts is uniform and applied in accounting. Generally, blocks of numbers are assigned to various groups of accounts. In most cases, a four-digit system is used in a business. In a four-digit system, the first digit refers to the major group in which the account is located. For example, 1 stands for assets; 2 for liabilities; 3 for common subjects; 4 for owner's equity; 5 for costs; 6 for profits and losses. The second digit designates

the position of the account in the group. The third and the fourth digits designate the account's specific title. Some accounting titles are listed as Exhibit 3-3 below.

Exhibit 3-3 The Chart of Accounts

Number	Title	Number	Title
1	Assets	3001	Liquidation of inter-bank business
1001	Cash on hand	3002	Currency exchange
1002	Cash in bank	3101	Derivative instruments
1111	Notes receivable	3201	Hedging instruments
1122	Accounts receivable	3202	Hedged items
1221	Other receivables	4	Owner's Equity
1401	Supplies purchasing	4001	Paid-in capital
1403	Raw materials	4002	Capital reserves
1405	Commodity stocks	4101	Surplus reserves
1601	Fixed assets	4103	Income summary
1602	Accumulated depreciation	4104	Profit distribution
1604	Construction in process	5	Costs
1701	Intangible assets	5001	Manufacturing cost
1801	Long-term deferred and prepaid expenses	5101	Manufacturing overheads
1901	Wait-deal assets loss or income	6	Profits and losses
2	Liabilities	6001	Prime operating revenue
2001	Short-term loans	6051	Other operating revenue
2201	Notes payable	6111	Investment income
2202	Accounts payable	6301	Non-operating income
2203	Prepayments by customers	6401	Operating costs
2211	Payables to employees	6402	Other operating costs
2221	Taxes and surcharges payable	6403	Tax and associate charges
2231	Interest payable	6601	Selling expenses
2232	Dividends payable	6602	Administrative expenses

Number	Title	Number	Title
2501	Long-term loans	6603	Financial expenses
3	Common Subjects	6711	Non-business expenditure

In western countries, some accountants prefer to assign numbers to accounts in alphabetical order, although this procedure is not a requirement of good accounting practice. In expense accounts, the preferred sequence is to assign numbers in the order of anticipated dollar amounts. Therefore, the account expected to have the largest amount (e.g. Rent Expense) is assigned as the first number, and other accounts follow in descending order. Miscellaneous Expense is generally assigned as the last number, even though it may not always be the smallest amount.

3.2 Accounting Rules

3.2.1 Review Accounting Equation

Note that the accounting system reflects two basic aspects of a business enterprise: what it owns and what it owes. Assets are resources with future benefits that are owned or controlled by a company. These resources are expected to yield future benefits. Examples are cash, supplies, equipment, and land. The claims on a company's assets-what it owns-are separated into owner and creditor claims. Liabilities are what a company owes its creditors in future payments, products, or services. Owner's equity (also called equity or capital) refers to the claims of its owner (s). Together, liabilities and owner's equity are the source of funds to acquire assets. The financial condition or position of a business enterprise is represented by the relationship of assets, liabilities, and owner's equity, and is reflected in the following accounting equation: Assets=Liabilities +Owner's Equity

According to the accounting equation, a firm is assumed to possess its assets subject to the rights of the creditors and owners.

A corporation's equity—often called stockholders' or shareholders' equity—

has two parts: contributed capital and retained earnings. Contributed capital refers to the amount that stockholders invest in the company—included under the title common stock. Retained earnings refer to income (revenues less expenses) that is not distributed to its stockholders. The distribution of assets to stockholders is called dividends, which reduce retained earnings. Revenues increase retained earnings and are the assets earned from a company's earning activities. Examples are consulting services provided, sales of products, facilities rented to others, and commissions from services. Expenses decrease retained earnings and are the cost of assets or services used to earn revenues. Examples are costs of employee time, use of supplies, and advertising, utilities, and insurance services from others. In sum, retained earnings are the accumulated revenues less the accumulated expenses and dividends since the company began. This breakdown of equity yields the following expanded accounting equation:

$$\text{Assets}=\text{Liabilities} + \text{Contributed Capital} + \text{Retained Earnings}$$
$$\text{Assets}=\text{Liabilities} +\text{Common Stock} - \text{Dividends} + \text{Revenues} - \text{Expenses}$$

A net income occurs when revenues exceed expenses. Net income increases equity. A net loss occurs when expenses exceed revenues, which decreases equity.

3.2.2 Accounting Rules for Assets, Liabilities and Equity

(1) Asset accounts: Asset accounts carry their balances forward from one period to the next. The left side of asset accounts is used for recording increases and the right side is used for recording decreases. Examples of asset accounts include Cash, Receivables, Prepaid expenses, Equipment, Buildings, and Land.

(2) Liability accounts: Liability accounts also carry their balances forward from one period to the next. The right side of liability accounts is used for recording increases and the left side is used for recording decreases. Examples of liability accounts are Payables, Unearned revenues and other liabilities (salaries, taxes, interest).

(3) Equity accounts: The balance in the equity accounts carries forward to the next accounting period. A separate account is employed for each item affecting equity-investments, withdrawals, income, and expenses.

(4) Capital/paid-in capital and retained earnings account: For a sole proprietorship, a capital account is used to record the original investment and any permanent additional increases or decreases in owner's equity. The right side of the capital account is used for recording increases and naturally the left side is used for recording decreases. For a corporation, a paid-in capital account is used for investment and retained earnings for undistributed profits.

(5) Withdrawa / dividend account: Withdrawal account (also known as a drawing account) is not a salary or an expense of the business. Owner's withdrawals of earnings or anticipated earnings include withdrawals of cash (or other assets) to pay personal expenses. Withdrawals are a distribution of earnings rather than an expense. They should be deducted from owner's equity directly. For a corporation, a dividend account is used and deducted from retained earnings (undistributed profits).

3.2.3 Accounting Rules for Revenue (both revenue and gains) and Expenses

The income statement accounts have balances only during an accounting period. The theory of debit and credit in its application to income and expense accounts is based on the relationship of these accounts to equity.

Income increases equity. These increases in income during an accounting period are recorded as credits. Expenses have the effect of decreasing equity, and these increases in expense accounts are recorded as debits.

Periodically, usually at the end of the accounting year, all income and expense accounts balances are transferred to a summarizing account and the accounts are then said to be closed, which are sometimes called temporary accounts or nominal accounts. The balance in the summarizing account, which is the net profit or net loss for the period, is then transferred to the capital account (to the retained earnings account for a corporation). The balances of the accounts reported in the balance sheet are carried forward from year to year and because of their permanence are sometimes referred to as real accounts.

Examples of income accounts include revenues from sales, repairs, commissions earned, rent earned, and interest earned. Examples of expense accounts include advertising expenses, office supplies expenses, salaries expenses, rent expenses, utilities expenses, and insurance expenses, etc.

3.3 Theory of Double-Entry

3.3.1 Definition and Characteristics

The methods used to record economic transactions are single-entry system and double-entry system. The latter is considered as the heart of modern accounting, and now it is widely used all over the world. Based on the accounting equation, double-entry accounting means each transaction is recorded in at least two accounts with equal amounts. If more than two accounts are affected, the total of the debit entries must equal the total of the credit entries. Further, the creation of assets within an enterprise is always accompanied by the incurring of identical financial obligations, either to the proprietors of the enterprise (owner's equity) or to outside creditors (liabilities). The derivation of profit is always accompanied by an identical increase in the net assets (i.e. assets minus liabilities) of the enterprise. It is possible to see how double-entry accounting produces this equilibrium of results by ensuring that the equation holds good at all time.

The double-entry accounting is used by virtually every business organization, regardless of whether the company's accounting records are maintained manually or by computer. Today we have computer software programs like Quick Books that appear to be single-entry (like your checkbook), but are actually written in a double-entry format.

Accuracy is improved because the accounting equation must balance after each transaction. Luca Paciolio, an Italian monk, introduced double-entry accounting back in 1494. The reason that double-entry accounting has been in existence for over 500 years is because it ensures accuracy. By applying the double-entry accounting, accountants can locate many types of errors which might be made while maintaining accounting records.

3.3.2 The Symbol of Debit and Credit

In double-entry accounting, when debit and credit are used as the symbol of account entries, the method called debit-credit bookkeeping occurs. The T-account is the basic form of the double-entry system and debit-credit bookkeeping, with the debit on the left and the credit on the right.

To debit an account means to enter an amount on the left side of the account. To credit an account means to enter an amount on the right side of the account. The abbreviation for debit is Dr. and for credit Cr. (based on the Latin terms debere and credere). Some times the word charge is used as a substitute for debit. In entering transactions, the debits must always equal the credits.

3.3.3 The Rules of Debit and Credit

The rules of debit and credit are based on the location of the basic elements in the accounting equation. Since left means debit in accounting and assets are on the left side of the equation, increases in assets are entered on the left or debit side of an account. Decreases in assets are entered on the right or credit side. Liabilities and owner's equity are on the right side of the accounting equation. Increases are entered on the right or credit side of an account. Decreases in liabilities or owner's equity are entered on the left or debit side. By following these rules, the basic equality of assets to equities (Assets=Liabilities + Owner's Equity) will be maintained.

The rules of debit and credit can be depicted with T-accounts, as follows:

Assets		=	Liabilities		+	Owner's Equity	
Debit for	Credit for		Debit for	Credit for		Debit for	Credit for
increases	decreases		decreases	increases		decreases	increases
Total Debits		=	**Total Credits**				

Owner's equity has separate accounts for owner's investments, withdrawals, revenues, and expenses.

Owner's Equity

Debit	Credit
(decreases)	(increases)
Withdrawals by owner	Investments by owner
(withdrawals account/dividends account)	(capital account/paid-in capital account)
	Undistributed profits
	(retained earnings account)
Expenses	Revenues
(expense accounts)	(revenue accounts)

The normal balance of each type of account is a debit or credit balance depending on which side of the account is used to record increases.

For example, someone started his company with $200 000 that was immediately deposited into the bank. This transaction shall be recorded below:

Debit	Cash in Bank	Credit
	200 000	

Debit	Paid-in Capital	Credit
	200 000	

Accordingly, an accounting entry for the transaction shall be made:

Dr. Cash in bank	$200 000
Cr. Paid-in capital	$200 000

3.3.4 Enter Business Transactions

(1) Use of asset, liability, and owner's equity accounts: The next step in learning accounting is to combine the accounting equation with the rules of debit and credit. We will review the same transactions for Peter Jonathan, a dentist, using T-accounts.

Transaction a: Peter Jonathan started a business by investing $30 000 in cash

Cash			Peter Jonathan, Capital	
(a) 30 000				(a) 30 000

Analysis: The asset Cash and Andy's equity in the business increased. Since Cash is an asset and assets are on the left side of the accounting equation, the Cash account was increased by a debit. Peter Jonathan, Capital, is on the right side of the equation and to show an increase in this account, Peter Jonathan, Capital, was credited for $30 000.

Transaction b: Andy purchased office equipment for $2 500 on account.

Office Equipment			Accounts Payable	
(b) 2 500				(b) 2 500

Analysis: To show an increase in the asset account, Office Equipment, it was debited for $2 500. Since liabilities are on the right side of the equation, increases to liabilities are shown on the right or credit side of the account. To increase the liabilities of the business, Accounts Payable was credited for $2 500.

Transaction c: Andy purchased office supplies for cash, $350.

Cash			Office Supplies	
(a) 30 000	(c) 350		(c) 350	

Analysis: One asset was increased while another asset was decreased. There is no change in total assets. Office Supplies were debited for the increase and Cash was credited for the decrease of $350. Office supplies are an asset at the time of purchase even though they will become an expense when used. The procedure used in accounting for supplies will be discussed later.

Transaction d: Andy paid $500 on account to the company from which the office equipment was purchased

Cash			Accounts Payable	
(a) 30 000	(c) 350 (d) 500		(d) 500	(b) 2 500

Analysis: The liability Accounts Payable was decreased with a debit, and the asset Cash was decreased with a credit for $500.

Transaction e: Purchased office supplies on account, $400

Office Supplies			Accounts Payable	
(c) 350 (e) 400			(d) 500	(b) 2 500 (e) 400

Analysis: The asset Office Supplies was increased with a debit. The liability Accounts Payable was increased with a credit. Assets are on the left or debit side of the accounting equation, and increases to assets are shown on the debit side of the account. Likewise, liabilities are on the right or credit side of the equation, and increases to liabilities are shown on the right or credit side of the account.

Transaction f: Andy withdrew $300 for personal use

Cash			Peter Jonathan, Drawing	
(a) 30 000	(c) 350 (d) 500 (f) 300		(f) 300	

Analysis: To decrease the asset account, Cash was credited for $300. Remember, a separate account, Peter Jonathan, Drawing, is used to accumulate withdrawals by the owner. Therefore, to decrease owner's equity, the drawing account was debited.

(2) Use of revenue and expense accounts: Revenue and expense accounts are to accumulate increases and decreases in owner's equity. By having a separate account for each type of revenue and expense, a clear record can be kept. Also, revenues and expenses can be kept separate from additional investments and withdrawals by the owner. The relationship of these accounts to owner's equity and the rules of debit and credit are indicated in the following diagram:

All Owner's Equity Accounts

Debit to enter Decreases (-) All Expense Accounts		Credit to enter Increases (+) All Revenue Accounts	
Debit to enter increases (+)	Credit to enter decreases (-)	Debit to enter decreases (-)	Credit to enter increases (+)

To illustrate the effect that revenue and expense accounts have on the double-entry process, we will continue to analyze the transactions of Peter Jonathan, a dentist, using T-accounts.

Transaction g: Received $4 500 in cash from a client for professional services rendered

Cash				Professional Fees	
(a) 30 000	(c) 350				(g) 4 500
	(d) 500				
(g) 4 500	(f) 300				

Analysis: This transaction increased the asset Cash, with an equal increase in owner's equity, because of revenue. The asset account Cash was debited and the revenue account Professional Fees was credited. Professional Fees is a temporary account that has the overall effect of increasing owner's equity.

Transaction h: Paid $1 500 for office rent for one month

Cash				Rent Expense	
(a)30 000	(c)350			(h)1 500	
	(d)500				
	(f)300				
(g)4 500	(h)1 500				

Analysis: This transaction decreased the asset Cash, with an equal decrease in owner's equity because of expense. Rent Expense was debited and Cash was credited for $1 500. Rent Expense is a temporary account that has the overall effect of decreasing owner's equity.

Transaction i: Paid bill for telephone service, $67

Cash			Telephone Expense	
(a)30 000	(c)350		**(i)67**	
	(d)500			
	(f)300			
(g)4 500	(h)1 500			
	(i)67			

Analysis: This transaction is identical to the previous one. Telephone Expense was debited and Cash was credited for $67.

Chapter 4   Accounting Vouchers and Accounting Books

Learning Objectives:

(1) Understand how to fill accounting vouchers.

(2) Understand how to set up journals.

(3) Understand how to set up ledgers.

In accounting practice, it is the first step for accountants to draw up and examine accounting vouchers. The vouchers include source documents and recording vouchers (or entry documents). They, on the basis of account book entries, are valid and written documents recording the occurrence and conclusion of each economic transaction, and certifying the economic responsibilities of the relevant staff. So it is required that the accounting information recorded should be authentic, accurate and complete. There are some regulations on when and how to submit accounting vouchers. At the end of an accounting period, these vouchers shall be properly kept in files as important accounting archives.

On the basis of the examined accounting vouchers, account book entries shall be conducted. Account books are carriers of recording accounting information and the database of collecting and keeping economic transactions. It is considered the center of accounting practice to set up and enter the account books, which are often sorted into journals and ledgers. In order to ensure the records in account books are accurate, the system of account reconciliation or verification shall be established, and accounts or entries shall be closed or balanced regularly. When errors occur in bookkeeping, corrections shall be made immediately. As important accounting archives, account books shall be properly kept in files.

4.1 Accounting Vouchers

4.1.1 The Definition of Accounting Vouchers

Accounting voucher is the collective name of source document and recording voucher, which is a document used to record the occurrence and completion of transactions or events, to clarify financial responsibility, and to register the books of accounts accordingly. Legally obtained, properly completed and reviewed vouchers are one of the specialized methods of accounting. The definition of accounting vouchers is shown in Figure 4-1.

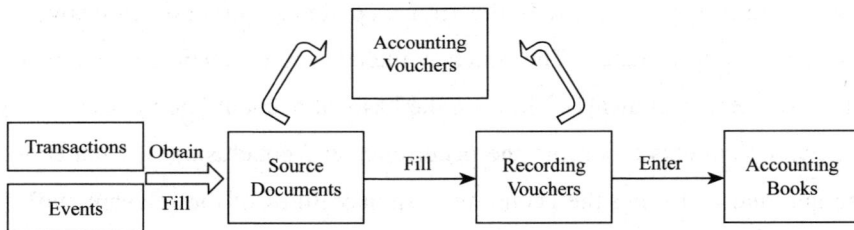

Figure 4-1　The Definition of Accounting Vouchers

According to the different preparation procedures and purposes, accounting vouchers can be divided into two types: source documents and recording vouchers. Source documents are original documents obtained or filled out by business operators or accountants when transactions or events occur or are completed, which are used to record or prove the occurrence and completion of transactions or events, and are important accounting information. In order to meet the requirements of bookkeeping, accountants should fill out recording vouchers based on the source documents that have been examined and cleared. Recording voucher is an accounting voucher that is prepared after the transactions or events are categorized according to their contents and the accounting entries are determined accordingly, and it is the direct basis for registering the books of accounts. Both the source document and the recording voucher must be signed or sealed by the person concerned in order to clarify the financial responsibility. The books of accounts recording transactions or events are mainly registered according to the recording vouchers, and some books of accounts also need to refer to the source documents for registration. Thus, accounting vouchers are the supporting documents on the basis of which the books of account are registered.

4.1.2 The Role of Accounting Vouchers

(1) Accounting voucher is an important vehicle for providing information on transactions or events. After any transaction or matter occurs, the person who handles the transaction or matter or the accountant must obtain or fill out accounting vouchers (i.e. source documents), which are the original information necessary for accounting. When the person in charge sends the relevant source document to the accounting department, the accountant will understand the content of the transaction or matter from it and determine the reasonable accounting treatment only after the necessary review. As you can see, accounting vouchers are an important vehicle for transmitting economic information. Even if some source documents are filled by accountants themselves, they need to be transmitted and exchanged among the accountants concerned, and this process is the process of transaction or matter processing.

(2) Accounting vouchers are the necessary basis for registering books of accounts. The accountant processes the accounting vouchers obtained to record the content of the transaction or event and fills in the recording vouchers (prepares accounting entries) on this basis to determine the accounts, directions and amounts to be registered for the business, so that the transactions or events occurring can be registered in the relevant accounts. Since accounting accounts are opened in the books of accounts, the registration of the books of accounts is also the registration of

the relevant accounts. As you can see, accounting vouchers are an important basis for registering books of accounts.

(3) Accounting vouchers are an important means to clarify financial responsibility. The transactions or matters that occur in the accounting subject are handled by the relevant personnel. The person who handles the transaction must sign or stamp on the accounting voucher when he/she completes certain aspects of the business. This can clarify the economic responsibility of the person or department who handles the transaction, and it is easy to find out if there is a mistake in handling the business. In addition, the transmission of accounting vouchers can also closely link the business departments and personnel within the unit, so that the relevant departments and personnel can check and control each other, and identify and deal with problems in a timely manner.

(4) Auditing accounting vouchers are the implementation of accounting supervision of specific measures. By reviewing the content of transactions or events reflected in accounting vouchers, accountants can check the authenticity, legality and compliance of the transactions or events, so that the transactions and events entered into the accounting information processing system meet the prescribed requirements and ensure the quality of accounting information from the source, and can timely identify problems in management and loopholes in the management system. Therefore, timely measures can be taken to deal with them, prevent problems before they occur, protect the security and integrity of enterprise property, and safeguard the economic interests of the parties concerned.

4.1.3 The Importance of Accounting Vouchers in Accounting Cycle

Accounting vouchers are one of the accounting methods. From the whole process of accounting cycle, it can be seen that the process of accounting cycle is the process of accounting and reporting the transactions or events occurring in the enterprise. Among them, the first six links belong to the accounting record link, and the methods used in accounting are mainly account setting, double-entry bookkeeping, voucher filling and bookkeeping; the seventh link belongs to the accounting report link, and the method of report preparation is used. The accounting record is the daily record of the transactions or events that occur in the enterprise, and the final record of certain events that are adjusted at the end of the accounting period; the accounting report is the processing and summarizing of all the information of the transactions or events that occur in the enterprise at the end of the accounting period.

Among the above accounting records and accounting reporting methods, the method of obtaining or filling accounting vouchers is the primary method of performing the processing of transactions or events. In every accounting cycle, it is always the key link in the chain of accounting cycle, which is indispensable for the preparation and acquisition of accounting vouchers, and is also the basic link for other links to be carried out smoothly. If this link is missing, the registration of accounting books and the preparation of accounting reports will not be possible. The obtaining and filling of accounting vouchers can provide a direct basis for the registration of accounting books (accounting records) and, accordingly, provide quality assurance for the preparation of accounting reports. Thus, accounting vouchers have an important place in the accounting cycle. The position of the accounting voucher method in the accounting cycle is shown in Figure 4-2.

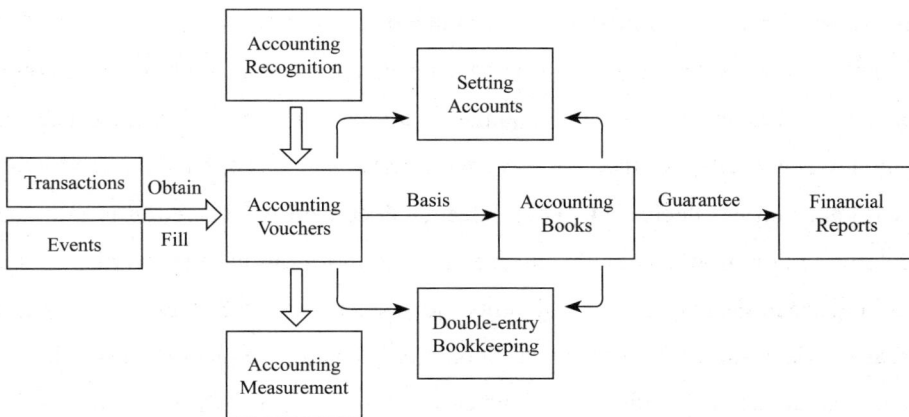

Figure 4-2 The Importance of Accounting Vouchers in Accounting Cycle

Certainly, methods such as account setting and double-entry bookkeeping are used in the process of accounting cycle. These methods are the ones that provide technical support for the preparation of accounting vouchers and the registration of books of accounts, etc. If a complete account system is not set up and the theoretical guidance of double-entry bookkeeping and the application of specific methods lack, the preparation of accounting vouchers and the registration of books of accounts will not be realized effectively. Accounting report is the continuation of accounting records, and accounting report is a specific method to summarize the accounting records comprehensively and to provide financial information such as financial status, operating results and cash flow of the enterprise. Without the method of accounting report to summarize and report the information formed by accounting records, the accounting information collected and accumulated by the accounting records link will become meaningless. As can be seen, methods such as accounting records and accounting reports are a complete system of accounting methods that should be used in conjunction with each other in the accounting cycle.

4.2 Source Documents

The accounting cycle begins with an analysis of source documents—A piece of paper or source of information that contains data that affects the business such as a receipt, invoice, sales ticket, or cash register tape. A careful study of each source document will determine which accounts are affected. For example, a cash receipt for money spent tells you that some account, perhaps an asset, has increased, while the cash account has decreased. When a source document is received, it is examined to determine how it affects the business's financial position, in other words, does all asset increase or decrease? Does a liability increase or decrease? Does owner's equity increase or decrease? After each transaction, the accounting equation must still be in balance (assets equal liabilities plus owner's equity). Source documents are original documents that record the occurrence and completion of economic transactions. They are filled in or got by the business clerks as soon as the transactions happen. When an economic transaction takes place, the business man writes accounting source documents, one for stub, one for the opposite and the last one for the accountant, e.g., invoices. There are some general elements in source documents including:

(1) Name of the document.

(2) Name of a company or department by which it's prepared.

(3) Date and numbers.

(4) Name of a company or person that receives the documents.

(5) Contents, such as digest of the transaction, amount, price and sum.

(6) Clerk's signature or signature.

Because of their different origins, we often see two kinds of source documents in use, namely the external source documents and the internal source documents. According to different filling methods and procedures, they can be classified into one-off documents, accumulation documents and summary documents. Their different formats also help us sort them into general source documents (e.g., commercial bills, payment receipt, etc.) and special source documents (e.g., stores requisition, travel expense form, etc.). Because a source document is the original record containing the details to substantiate a transaction entered in an accounting system, it shall be filled in at the right time with authentic and complete items and accurate amounts. At the same time, it is written in accordance with laws and regulations. During an auditing, source documents are used as the evidence that a particular business transaction occurred, so we always consider whether they are legal, reasonable, complete, authentic or timely.

4.3 Recording Vouchers

Recording vouchers are also called entry documents. They are drawn up by accounting personnel based on the examined source documents or documents'summaries. According to these entry documents, seen as important accounting vouchers, accounting entries and account books can be made directly. A recording voucher plays the role of a medium between the source document and the account book, changing the data in the source document into the accounting language for journals and ledgers. According to different transactions recorded, recording vouchers can be divided into general vouchers and special vouchers. Special vouchers contain three kinds, i.e. receipt vouchers, disbursement vouchers and transfer vouchers depending on whether the recorded transaction has the money or not. Recording vouchers have different formats and can be also classified into single entry documents and double-entry documents.

As soon as an economic transaction occurs, the recording voucher shall be filled in legibly with authentic record, complete content and proper procedures. In addition, when filling, accounting personnel are required to obey the following rules:

(1) A suitable type of voucher shall be chosen.

(2) Explanation or description on the transaction should be expressed briefly.

(3) Accounting entry shall be made in accordance with the account.

(4) Vouchers shall be numbered sequentially.

(5) Vouchers may not be arbitrarily compiled or separated.

(6) Pages of the vouchers shall be marked exactly.

(7) An error in the voucher should be filled.

(8) The column of amount shall be filled in according to the regulations, and blanks should be crossed off with a line.

(9) Recording vouchers computerized must also conform to the uniform standard.

Accordingly, when accountants audit recording vouchers, they try to discover:

(1) Whether the vouchers are prepared on the basis of the examined source documents.

(2) Whether proper accounts are applied.

(3) Whether amounts are correct and accurate.

(4) Whether accounting procedures are undertaken.

4.3.1 Receipt Vouchers

In the top left-hand corner of the receipt voucher, Cash on hand or Cash in a bank shall be filled in as the debit's title. The date in the middle and its sequential number in the right corner are written down too. In the description column, a brief reason for recording the transaction is included. In the credit column, its accounting titles (i.e. , the general and subsidiary) in accordance with the received cash or cash in bank are filled in. Posting reference (P. R.) is marked too so that no transaction is recorded more than once or left out. The exact figure incurred by the transaction, pages of source documents attached and relevant persons'seals at the bottom are all contained. See Exhibit 4-1 below.

Exhibit 4-1 Receipt Voucher

Debit			

Date   No. _____

Description	Credit		Amount	P. R.	Attachment page (s)
	General	Subsidiary			
Total					

Supervised by (seal) Entered by (seal) Handled by (seal) Checked by (seal) Filled by (seal)

4.3.2 Disbursement Vouchers

The disbursement voucher is drawn up almost in the same way as the receipt voucher, but in its top left-hand corner the credit's title shall be filled in with Cash on hand or Cash in the bank. The second column is the debit, and its accounting titles (i.e. the general and subsidiary) in conformity with the disbursed cash or cash in the bank are filled in. Exhibit 4-2 is shown below.

Exhibit 4-2 Disbursement Voucher

Credit	

Date _____ No. _____

Description	Debit		Amount	P. R.	Attachment page (s)
	General	Subsidiary			
Total					

Supervised by (seal) Entered by (seal) Handled by (seal) Checked by (seal) Filled by (seal)

4.3.3 Transfer Vouchers

In the transfer voucher, accounting titles with the general and subsidiary shall be individually filled in according to the debit's and credit's accounts. The figure of the credit and the sum of the debit are entered in the amount column. We can refer to the following sample. Please note here that recording vouchers for general purposes are drawn up almost in the same way as transfer vouchers (See Exhibit 4-3).

Exhibit 4-3 Transfer Voucher

Date _____ No. _____

Description	General	Subsidiary	Amount Debited	Amount Credited	P. R.	Attachment page (s)
Total						

Supervised by (seal) Entered by (seal) Checked by (seal) Filled by (seal)

For example, on November 21 2022, Shanhai Company sent ABC Company a transfer check, paying 56 500 yuan for the goods that it once bought. ABC Company saved the money in the bank. Then the receipt voucher shall be filled in as Exhibit 4-4 below.

Exhibit 4-4   Receipt Voucher

Debit	Cash in bank

November 21, 2022 No. 28

Description	Credit		Amount	P. R.	Attachment 2 page (s)
	General	Subsidiary			
Payment of the goods sold	Accounts Receivable	Shanhai Co.	56 500		
Total (Capital in Chinese)			¥ 56 500		

Supervised by (seal) Entered by (seal) Handled by (Wang) Checked by (Wu) Filled by (Jia)

4.4 Transmission and Maintenance of Accounting Vouchers

4.4.1 Transmission of Accounting Vouchers

Transmission of accounting vouchers refers to the procedure of transmission of accounting vouchers between relevant departments and personnel within the enterprise from obtaining, filling, using to filing and keeping.

Accounting vouchers are the basis for transactions or events, which determines the fluidity of accounting vouchers among relevant functional departments and personnel.

The transmission procedure of accounting vouchers varies with the content of transactions or matters occurring in enterprises, but the following aspects should be noted in the transmission of accounting vouchers.

(1) An orderly transmission route should be determined. The transmission route of accounting vouchers refers to the flow of vouchers through the link and sequence, based on the specific content of the transaction or matter and processing requirements, to determine a reasonable and orderly voucher transmission route, so that accounting vouchers move along the fastest and most reasonable flow of operation, It not only ensures that the handling personnel can be timely transaction or matter processing and accounting personnel for account processing, but also avoids voucher transmission "offside", not to mention that the transmission of vouchers should not be made to go through unnecessary links.

(2) Reasonable transmission time should be clarified. The transmission time refers to the time that the accounting voucher stays in the hands of the relevant department or personnel. The stay time of accounting vouchers in the hands of relevant departments or personnel should be reasonably determined according to the needs of each link in dealing with transactions or matters, so as to ensure the timely transmission of accounting vouchers and avoid the stay time being too long and affecting the processing of the next link.

(3) Strict transmission procedures should be carried out. The procedure of passing accounting vouchers refers to the procedure that should be handled by the relevant departments or personnel in the process of handing over the vouchers. In order to avoid the loss or damage of accounting vouchers and eliminate the security risks in the process of passing accounting vouchers, the handover procedures should be handled in each link of voucher handover and the responsibilities of each link and relevant personnel should be clarified.

4.4.2 Maintenance of Accounting Vouchers

The maintenance of accounting vouchers mainly refers to the preservation and management of various accounting vouchers formed by an enterprise after a transaction or event has occurred. Accounting vouchers are important economic files and historical information of the enterprise, and measures should be taken to keep them properly. After the transactions or events reflected on the accounting vouchers are registered in the accounts, the accounting vouchers that have been used should be organized, bound and filed for investigation, and should not be lost or arbitrarily destroyed, so as to ensure the safety and integrity of the accounting vouchers. The storage period of accounting vouchers is generally 15 years. Accounting vouchers can be destroyed only after the expiration of the storage period in accordance with the provisions. The following links should be noted in the custody of accounting vouchers.

(1) Organize, categorize, and bind into a book. At the end of each month, enterprises should generally organize the recording vouchers that have been registered in this month, and bind them into a book according to the numbering order together with the attached source documents to prevent them from being lost. For an excessive number of source documents, you can also bind them separately for safekeeping. For future reference, a cover sheet should be added to the bound vouchers, indicating the name of the unit, the completion date of the vouchers, the type and quantity of accounting vouchers, etc., and signed or stamped by the person concerned.

(2) Make up an inventory and file it for safekeeping. At the end of an accounting year, the accounting department will compile and file the accounting vouchers in accordance with the requirements for filing. The current year's accounting vouchers can be kept by the accounting department for one year after the end of the year to facilitate the reconciliation and succession of inter-year transactions or events. After the expiration of the period, the accounting department shall compile an inventory and transfer it to the archives department of the unit for proper storage according to the archives'storage requirements.

(3) Proper storage and control of borrowing. Accounting documents in custody should be prevented from damage that may be caused by natural environment and

other factors, but also from damage and loss of human causes, etc., and should take effective measures to closely guard. In principle, accounting documents in custody shall not be lent, and must be reported to the head of the unit for approval for special needs. However, the original volume shall not be dismantled, and shall be returned by the deadline. Copies of source documents provided to the outside shall be registered in a special register and signed or stamped by the person providing and receiving them.

4.5 Preview of Accounting Books

4.5.1 Meanings of Accounting Books

An accounting book is also called an account book for short. Based on the examined accounting vouchers, it is the book that records all the economic transactions for an enterprise or a unit systematically and consecutively. Therefore, it always consists of relevant pages with specific forms.

4.5.2 Types of Accounting Books

Generally speaking, account books include journals (or daily books), ledgers (i. e, general ledgers and subsidiary ledgers), and other auxiliary account books (or memorandum). Sometimes they are classified into two-column books, three-column books, multi-column books and amount-type books. Among them three-column books are common in journals and ledgers. According to their different appearances, they are sorted into bound ledgers, loose-leaf ledgers and card account books. The account book contains its cover, title-page, pages and back cover, and in the pages, there are columns for the account title, date, voucher's type and order, digest and page order, etc.

When accountants enter account books, they shall obey the following rules and regulations:

(1) All the records shall be correct and complete.

(2) Signs for posting reference are marked.

(3) Words and figures are clear and accurate.

(4) They are normally entered in blue or black ink.

(5) Special records can be in red ink.

(6) They are entered with the order of pages consecutively numbered.

(7) The balance is calculated.

(8) At the end of a page, the words "Refer to the front or next page" are written down when necessary.

(9) Correction for any error shall be made in accordance with the stipulated methods, otherwise no scrape or modification is allowed.

4.6 Journals

In a western accounting system, the information about each business transaction is initially recorded in an accounting record called a journal. Afterward, the data is transferred or posted to the ledger, the book of subsequent or secondary entry. The various transactions are evidenced by sales tickets, purchase invoices, check stubs and so on. Since the journal is the accounting record in which transactions are first recorded, it is sometimes called the book of original entry. It is also called the day book because the journal is a chronological (day-by-day) record of all business transactions.

Technically speaking, it is possible to record transactions directly in the ledger, then why bother to maintain a journal? The answer is that the unit of organization for the journal is the transaction, whereas the unit of organization for the ledger is the account. By having both a journal and a ledger, we achieve several advantages which would not be possible if transactions were recorded directly in ledger accounts.

(1) The journal shows all information about a transaction in one place and also

provides an explanation of the transaction. In a journal entry, the debits and credits for a given transaction are recorded together, but when the transaction is recorded in the ledger, the debits and credits are entered in different accounts. Since a ledger may contain hundreds of accounts, it would be very difficult to locate all the facts about a particular transaction by looking in the ledger. The journal is the record which shows the complete story of a transaction in one entry.

(2) The journal provides a chronological record of all the financial events in the life of a business. If we want to look up the facts about a transaction of some months or years back, all we need is the date of the transaction in order to locate it in the journal.

(3) The use of a journal helps to prevent errors. If transactions were recorded directly in the ledger, it would be very easy to make errors such as omitting the debit or the credit, or entering the debit twice or the credit twice. Such errors are not likely to be made in the journal, since the offsetting debits and credits appear together for each transaction.

Many businesses maintain several types of journals. The nature of operation and the volume of transactions in the particular business determine the number and type of journals needed. Journals are designed to record information about different transactions, including sales, purchases, cash receipts and cash disbursements, and many others. Journals have two or more columns to record increases or decreases in the accounts affected by the transaction, and they often have space for a date and an explanation of the transaction. They may be grouped into general journals and specialized journals.

4.6.1 General Journals

The simplest type of journal is called a general journal. It has only two money columns, one for debits and the other for credits. It may be used for all types of transactions. First the debit and then the credit of each transaction are recorded in the general journal. In addition, a brief explanation of the transaction is given. For example, an asset (Cash) account may increase while a liability account (Notes Payable) increases, indicating that money is borrowed and the business will repay it.

The general journal is also called a book of original entry because it is where the first accounting record of a transaction is made from a source document. The two-column general journal illustrated in Exhibit 4-5, is the simplest form of journal used in business. General journal pages are numbered consecutively.

Exhibit 4-5 General Journal

Page

	Date	Account title & Explanation	Post. Ref.	Debit	Credit	
1						1
2						2
3						3
4						4
5						5

(1) The date column. The year is written once at the first line, together with the month and day. After the first entry, only the day is written until the beginning of the next month's entries.

(2) Accounts that are affected by each transaction are written in the description column. A separate line is used for each account title (such as Cash and Accounts Payable). This column may also include a brief reason for the journal entry.

(3) The posting reference column (Post. Ref.). This column provides a cross-reference between the journal and the general ledger accounts. Entries in this column are made when journal entries are posted to the ledger accounts.

(4) The debit column. The amount being debited to an account is listed in this column.

(5) The credit column. The amount being credited to an account is listed in this column.

4.6.2 Special Journals

In the modern world, a business of any size enters into so many transactions that the use of a single journal would impose intolerable restrictions on its ability to maintain adequate records. It is, therefore, usual to break down or subdivide the journal into a number of specialized journals, each being used to record transactions of a certain kind. It is much simpler and more efficient to group together those transactions that are repetitive such as sales, purchases, cash receipts and cash payments and place each of them in a special journal. Therefore, the following special journals may be established:

(1) Sales journal: It is used to record sales on credit. As for cash sales, they are written in the cash receipts & disbursements journal. When a sales journal is used, posting labor is saved by waiting until the end of month totaling the numerous sales recorded in it (Exhibit 4-6).

Exhibit 4-6　Sales Journal

Date	Accounts debited	Post. Ref.	Amounts
3.1	Kotter Company		$20 000
3.4	Rob Club		$13 000
3.15	John Service Co.		$21 000
3.23	Rob Club		$40 000

(2) Purchase journal: In this journal, the accounts payable column is used to record the amounts of credits to each creditor's account. These amounts are posted daily to the individual creditor's accounts in the accounts payable subsidiary ledger. The column total represents an entry to be made at the end of the month (Exhibit 4-7).

Exhibit 4-7　Sales Journal

Date	Accounts debited	Terms	Post. Ref.	Amounts
3.3	ABC Company			$15 000
3.12	RPD Co.			$83 000

Date	Accounts debited	Terms	Post. Ref.	Amounts
3.19	Green Station			$34 000
3.28	ABC Company			$10 000

(3) Cash receipts & disbursements journal: Cash is such an important asset that it is necessary to establish a special journal to record cash receipts and disbursements. The cash receipts of a business differ as to their sources. They normally fall into three groups: cash from cash sales; cash from charge customers in payment of their accounts; cash from all the sources other than the above two sources. Similar to the cash receipts, cash disbursements also have repetitive debits and credits of cash payments, which are debits to accounts payable and credits to both purchase discount and cash (Exhibit 4-8).

Exhibit 4-8　Cash Receipts & Disbursements Journal

Date	Accounts debited(credited)	Explanation	Post. Ref.	Debit	Credit	Balance
3.1	Capital			$90 000		$90 000
3.8	Rent Expense				3 000	$87 000
3.16	Sales			$20 000		$107 000
3.22	Wages Payable				3 400	$103 600

(4) Cash on hand & cash in bank journal: In China, cash on hand journals and cash in bank journals are more widely used than others. Cash on hand journal is applied in a company to conduct accounting and supervision on the cash on hand concerning daily receipt, disbursement and balance. There are some main columns for the date, document's type and order, digest, opposite account, debit, credit and balance, etc. For the document's type, we can fill in with "cash receipt", "cash payment", "bank deposit receipt" or "bank deposit payment". Cash in bank journal is the journals used for daily cash in bank, and it is entered almost in the same way as cash on hand journals. Refer to Exhibit 4-9 and Exhibit 4-10.

Exhibit 4-9   Cash on Hand Journal

2022 Year		Document		Digest	Opposite Account	Debit	Credit	Balance
Month	Date	Type	No.					
Mar.	1st			Opening balance				$7 000
Mar.	1st	Cash receipt	1	Withdrawal for use	Cash in bank	$300		$6 700
Mar.	1st	Cash payment	2	Expense for water and electricity	Administrative expenses	$2 000		$4 700
Mar.	1st	Cash payment	15	Payment for wages	Wages payable	$700		$4 000
Total								$4 000

Exhibit 4-10   Cash in Bank Journal

2022 Year		Document		Digest	Opposite Account	Debit	Credit	Balance
Month	Date	Type	No.					
Mar.	1st			Opening balance				$5 000
Mar.	3rd	Bank deposit payment	1	Withdrawal for use	Cash on hand	$400		$4 600
Mar.	5th	Bank deposit receipt	3	Receipt from accounts receivable	Accounts receivable	$2 000		$6 600
Mar.	12th	Bank deposit payment	15	Payment for wages	Wages payable	$1 500		$5 100
Total								$5 100

Advantages of Special Journals

① Reduce detailed recording. Each sales transaction is recorded on a single line with all details included on that line: date, customer's name, and amount.

② Reduce posting. There is only one posting made to accounts receivable and one posting to sales, regardless of the number of transactions.

③ Permit better division of labor. If there are several journals, it makes it possible for more than one bookkeeper to work on the books at the same time.

4.7 Ledgers

As was mentioned earlier, an account is a record of the changes and balances in the value of an individual item of an organization. It is understandable that an enterprise may use a number of accounts. The complete set of accounts for a business entity is called a ledger. It is the "reference book" of the accounting system and is used to classify and summarize transactions and to prepare data for financial statements. It is also a valuable source of information for managerial purposes, giving, for example, the amount of sales for the period or the cash balance at the end of the period. While most companies' ledgers contain similar accounts, a company often uses one or more unique accounts because of its type of operations.

4.7.1 General Ledger

General ledger is set up in accordance with the accounts of general ledger and classified to record economic activities by business, which provide general accounting information. A general ledger contains a specific account for each item listed on the financial statements and shows how each transaction changes the balances of these accounts. A company's size and diversity of operations affect the number of accounts needed. A small company can get as few as 20 or 30 accounts; a large company can require several thousand. It is desirable to establish a systematic method of identifying and locating each account in the ledger. The chart of accounts, sometimes called the code of accounts, is a listing of the accounts by title and numerical designation. It serves both as an index to the ledger and a description of the accounting system and also a link between financial statements and the ledger.

Accountants can enter the general ledger based on accounting voucher one by one, and can also use the categorized accounts summary or bookkeeping procedure using summary vouchers to enter directly.

4.7.2 Subsidiary Ledger

A large number of individual accounts with a common characteristic can be grouped together in a separate ledger called a subsidiary ledger. Each subsidiary ledger is represented in the general ledger by a summarizing account, called a controlling account. The sum of the balances of the accounts in a subsidiary ledger must equal the balance of the related controlling account. Subsidiary ledger is set up in accordance with the specific accounts and classified to record the economic activities with more detailed information.

Further, in subsidiary ledgers, for the accounts of fixed assets, debtor and creditor should be entered one by one; finished goods, raw materials can be entered one by one, or be summarized to enter periodically, and so do the accounts of revenue, expenses and costs. Formats of subsidiary ledger include three-column (such as "Accounts Receivable", refer to Exhibit 4-11), multi-column (such as "Manufacturing Cost", refer to Exhibit 4-12), amount-type (such as "Raw Materials", refer to Exhibit 4-13), horizontal-line (such as "Other Receivables", refer to Exhibit 4-14), etc.

Exhibit 4-11　Accounts Receivable Subsidiary Ledger

2022 Year		Document No.	Digest	Opposite Account	Debit	Credit	Dr. / Cr.	Balance
Month	Date							
3	1		Opening Balance				Dr.	485 313. 80
	13	4	Receipt from	Cash in Bank		485 313. 80		0
3	31		Total			485 313. 80		0

Exhibit 4-12 Manufacturing Cost Subsidiary Ledger

2022 Year		Document		Digest	Debit	Items of Cost		
Month	Date	Type	No.			Direct Materials	Direct Labor	Overhead
3	5	Transfer	3	Consumption of Raw Materials	117 800	117 800		
	31	Transfer	13	Allocation of Wages	42 000		42 000	
	31	Transfer	16	Allocation of Overhead	17 220			17 220
3	31			Total	177 020			
3	31	Transfer	17	Transfer Finished Product Cost	−177 020	−117 800	−42 000	−17 220
3	31			**Ending Balance**	0	0	0	0

Exhibit 4-13 Raw Materials Subsidiary Ledger

Material No. : 3001 unit: kilogram

Category: Raw and main materials storage: warehouse No. 1

Name of material: A storage ration: 4 000

2022 Year		Document		Digest	In			Out			Balance		
Month	Date	Type	No.		Number	Unit	Sum	Number	Unit	Sum	Number	Unit	Sum
3	1			Opening balance							300	20	6 000
	10	Transfer	8	Consumption				200	20	4 000	100	20	2 000
	31			Total				200	20	4 000	100	20	2 000

Exhibit 4-14 Other Receivables Subsidiary Ledger

2022 Year		Document No.	Digest	Debit			2022 Year		Document No.	Digest	Debit			Balance
Month	Date			Beginning	Renewal	Subtotal	Month	Date			Reimbursement	Return	Subtotal	
3	7	10	F. X.	600		600	8	12	90	Reimbursement	580	20	600	

Advantages of Subsidiary Ledgers

(1) Reduce ledger detail. Most of the information will be in the subsidiary ledger, and the general ledger will be reserved chiefly for summary or total figures. Therefore, it will be easier to prepare the financial statements.

(2) Permit better division of labor. Here, each special or subsidiary ledger may be handled by a different person. Therefore, one person may work on the general ledger accounts while another person may work simultaneously on the subsidiary ledger.

(3) Permit a different sequence of accounts. In the general ledger, it is desirable to have the accounts in the same sequence as in the balance sheet and income statement. As a further aid, it is desirable to use numbers to locate and refer to the accounts. However, in connection with accounts receivable, which involve names of customers or companies, it is preferable to have the accounts in an alphabetical sequence.

(4) Permit better internal control. Better control is maintained if a person other than the person responsible for the general ledger is responsible for the subsidiary ledger. For example, the trial balance of accounts receivable in the subsidiary ledger should agree with the balance of the accounts receivable account in the general ledger. The general ledger account acts as a controlling account, and the subsidiary ledger must agree with the control.

The Relationship Between General Ledger and Subsidiary Ledger

Between the general ledger and its subsidiary ledger, there is a special relationship that the balance of the general ledger is equal to the sum of balances in its subsidiary ledgers. So, for the same transaction that happens in the same period, it is required to record the same account and make the same debit and credit entries in the general ledger and subsidiary ledger. In other words, general ledger and its subsidiary ledger should enter it in parallel, and satisfy the following rules: the same evidence, the same direction, the same period and the same amounts. Both of them must be checked regularly.

Chapter 5 Main Business Transactions

Learning Objectives:

(1) To learn to make basic entries of accounting practice.

(2) To command the calculation of financial results.

In a business, the operating process can be made up of the supply process, the production process and the sales process, but funding is a prerequisite of its production and operating activities. When a business is set up, the owner must prepare enough funds for its normal operation. In order to calculate and supervise the funds' circulation, accounting personnel shall need to analyze the cost of purchasing goods, the cost of producing goods and the cost of selling goods. Therefore, it's necessary for them to master cost calculation methods. At the same time, they shall understand and master what constitutes the operating profit, total profit and net profit, how these items are formed, and how profits can be allocated according to relevant policies or regulations.

5.1 General Enterprises Concepts and Main Business Transactions or Events

5.1.1 The Definition of General Enterprises

General enterprises are those engaged in the production and sale of products, or only in the sale of goods and the provision of labor services as the main content of business activities. They include the organization of product production and sales of industrial enterprises (also known as manufacturing); the organization of commodity distribution of merchandising enterprises; as well as the provision of labor services as the main content of business activities of labor enterprises.

The enterprises, other than general enterprises, according to the characteristics of the industry can be called special enterprises. Special enterprises refer to certain special industries managed by the nature of the enterprise, such as commercial banks, insurance and securities industry.

The concept of general business and special business is shown in Figure 5-1.

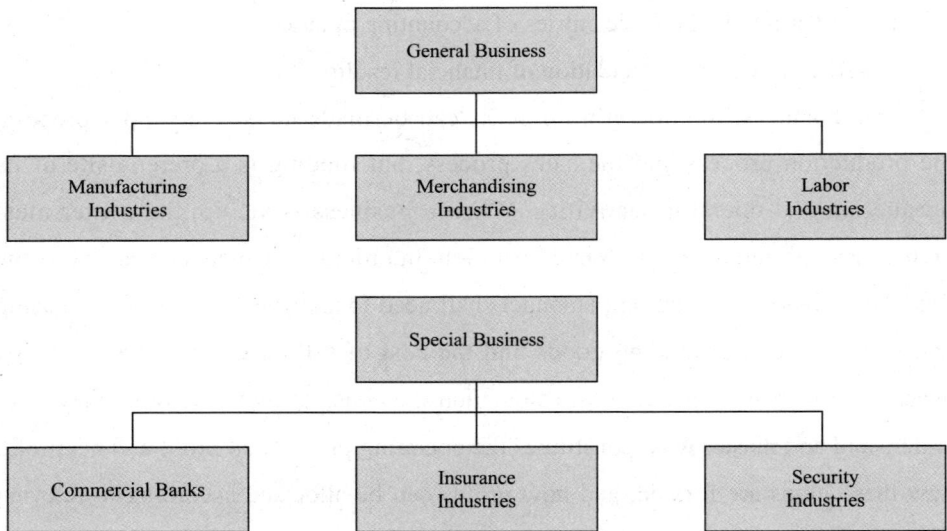

Figure 5-1   General Business and Special Business

The content of business activities of special enterprises is quite different compared with general enterprises. For example, for commercial banks, their business activities are mainly deposit-taking and loan issuance, etc. ; for insurance companies, their business activities are mainly to handle insurance business; for securities companies, their business activities are mainly dealing in securities and underwriting securities. Obviously, the business activities of general enterprises are different from these enterprises. In particular, product manufacturing enterprises are economic organizations whose main business activities are manufacturing and selling certain products, and their business activities are not only different from those of special enterprises, but also different from those of other general enterprises, such as commercial enterprises and service enterprises. There are many differences in the accounting treatment of transactions and events between production enterprises and other general and special enterprises.

5.1.2 Characteristics of General Enterprises

General enterprises, like commercial banks, insurance companies and securities companies, are economic organizations whose main business purpose is to make profits. Through the effective organization and management of production and operation activities, commodity circulation activities and labor service provision activities, enterprises strive to create more profits, which can, on the one hand, enhance their business performance, strengthen their development strength and provide strong support for their sustainable development; on the other hand, influence and drive the development of the local economy and pay more taxes and fees, and bear the social responsibility that enterprises should undertake. Finally, these business activities can also influence and drive the economic development of the region, and make due contribution to the harmonious development of society.

5.1.3 Main Business Transactions and Events of General Enterprises

(1) Fund collection business: Fund collection businesses are activities that lead to changes in the size and composition of the enterprise's capital and debt, and are an essential activity for enterprises to obtain operating funds and ensure the normal conduct of their business activities, as well as a prerequisite for conducting business

activities and investment activities. In modern enterprises, there are two main channels for enterprises to obtain operating funds: one is to attract investors to invest capital in enterprises; the other is to attract social investment through borrowing or issuing corporate bonds and other forms of debt. The capital invested here includes both paid-in capital (equity) and capital premium (equity premium); the debt raised here includes borrowing from banks, issuing bonds and repaying debts. The occurrence of these transactions and events will cause changes in the operating capital of the enterprise and the scale of debt, and therefore occurs in the financing activities of the enterprise. Normally, accounts payable and notes payable of enterprises are not transactions and events in financing activities, because they occur in the course of operating activities of enterprises and should be classified as transactions and events in operating activities.

(2) Supply process business: In product manufacturing companies, the supply process is the process of making necessary preparations for product production. The main purpose is to prepare labor objects such as materials and supplies, i.e., to purchase raw materials and main materials with the funds raised, to settle the payment for the suppliers of materials and supplies, to pay the price of materials and supplies, and to pay taxes and fees. There are cash and credit settlement methods for the settlement of payments. In the case of credit settlement, the enterprise will generate accounts payable and prepayment, etc., which form the settlement funds for the supply process. In addition, enterprises should also cost the various materials and supplies purchased in order to provide a basis for calculating the consumption of materials and supplies. Of course, the purchase and construction of buildings and equipment, etc. are also carried out in this process, but these activities belong to the investment activities of the enterprise, and the related contents are introduced in the section on investment activities' transactions and events and their accounting treatment.

(3) Production process business: During the production process, companies arrange the production of products according to product production plans or orders

from customers. A large number of transactions and events occurring in this process are expressed as consumption of operating funds. For example, carrying out product production consumes raw materials stocked in the supply process, consumes various fixed assets formed in investment activities; settling and paying salaries for production workers and management workers of the enterprise, etc., and paying various production expenses incurred with monetary funds involve consumption of the enterprise, etc. In the case that some payables are not paid temporarily, settlement funds in terms of payables will also be formed. When all the processes of product production are completed, finished products are formed. Enterprises should also calculate the cost of finished products and work-in-progress products produced in order to determine the various costs incurred in the production of the products and to provide a basis for setting the selling price of the products.

(4) Sales process business: The sales process is the process by which a company provides products to purchasers through the market or on order. The main transactions and events in this process are: settlement of the payment for the product with the customer, collection of the sale price and the taxes that should be charged. There are cash and credit settlements for the payment of goods. In the case of credit settlement, the enterprise generates accounts receivable and accounts receivable in advance, which form the settlement funds for the sales process. In addition, after the products are sold, the enterprise should perform the calculation of the cost of products sold in due course so that these costs can be matched with the revenue realized from the products sold to determine the results of product sales.

5.2 Accounting of Fund Collection Business

A business is always funded by its owner's investment and borrowed money from banks or other creditors. The former is named equity financing or paid-in capital, and the latter called debt financing becomes its debt. The owner's investment in a business will increase his (or her) equity and assets with the same amount. Loan from the bank is a typical kind of liability. When a company gets a loan, its assets and liabilities are increased with the same amount. So under the above conditions, the accounting equation will be kept in balance. Thus those accounts are designed, such as paid-in capital, loan from the bank, cash in the bank, interest payable, etc.

5.2.1 Equity Financing

As we learned before, owners' equity represents the owners' claims on the assets of the business. One of the primary sources to increase owners' equity is the investments of cash or other assets from the owners to the business. Investments to a business by the owners will increase both owners' equity and the relative assets, which will keep the accounting equation in balance.

In this chapter, we will illustrate this with detailed examples happening to Shanhai Company, a new toy manufacturing business. Furthermore, we will examine and record all the transactions happening to Shanhai Company in January 2022 as our examples.

On January 1, 2021, the Shanhai Company was established, and the owners invested $10 000 in cash, $32 000 in the form of patent X, and $50 000 in the form of equipment Y (assume VAT is not considered). In this case, the owner's assets and equity both increased by $92 000 at the same time. So in the entry, cash, patent and equipment should be debited as the assets account, and paid-in capital account should be credited.

So the owner's equity increased by $92 000 in total, and the entries should be as follows.

January 1, 2021	
Dr. Cash in bank	$10 000
Intangible assets—patent X	$32 000
Fix assets—equipment Y	$50 000
Cr. Paid-in capital	$92 000

Here, the owners invested some cash and non-cash assets to the business; therefore, cash, patent and equipment accounts were debited because all these assets were increased by the investment. Capital account was credited because owner's equity was increased at the same time.

5.2.2 Debt Financing

As we learned before, liability or debt represents debtees' claims on the assets of the business. It is another major source to get financed for a business besides equity financing.

A loan borrowed from bank is a typical kind of liability of a business. When getting a loan, both asset (cash) and liability (loan) are increased by the same amount, which keeps the both sides of the accounting equation in balance.

On January 1, 2022, Shanhai Company managed to borrow $12 000 from the bank with the annual interest rate of 10%. The term was one year, and the interest should be saved monthly at the end of each month. They agreed that the principal with its interest should be paid back as soon as the term was over.

Here because of the loan, the company's assets and liabilities both increased by $12 000 at the same time. In the entry of January 1, 2022, Shanhai Company should debit cash in the bank and credit short-term loans. Accordingly, in the entry of December 31, 2022, interest payable and short-term loans should be debited, and cash in bank should be credited. The following entries should be made.

Jan. 1, 2022	
Dr. Cash in bank	$12 000
Cr. Short-term loans	$12 000
Jan. 31, 2022	
Dr. Financial expenses—interest	$100
Cr. Interest payable	$100

Dec. 31, 2022	
Dr. Interest payable	$1 200
Short-term loans	$12 000
Cr. Cash in bank	$13 200

5.3 Accounting of Supply Process Business

For any manufacturing industry, supplying is the beginning of its operating activities. During the supplying process, it's necessary for the owners to spend certain money in building the factory and purchasing the machinery and materials. In this way, the assets needed for manufacturing should be prepared. Some of them could be invested by the owners, while more (e.g. materials especially) will be purchased during the operation. Accounting for Supplying means working out the funds for the purchase of fixed assets or raw materials, including the expenses and costs related to the assets or materials. So in order to conduct accounting and supervising on the supplying process, the accounts of assets and those of liabilities shall be designed. The former always includes fixed assets, raw materials, materials purchase and advances to suppliers, and the latter refers to accounts payable and taxes and surcharges payable.

5.3.1 Accounting for Raw Materials Purchasing

Raw materials are the basic materials and parts purchased for producing saleable products. Once the company purchases raw materials, they increase with cash decreased or accounts payable increased by the same amount. Usually, raw materials are on the debit side, and cash in bank or accounts payable are on the credit side.

On May 1, 2022, Shanhai Company spent $10 000 in purchasing materials from Company B and the value-added tax (VAT) was $1 300. The materials were received and stored in the warehouse after examination. On May 8, 2022, Shanhai Company paid the bill. Then it should record the entries as the following:

May 1, 2022	
Dr. Raw materials	$10 000
Taxes and surcharges payable—VAT payable (input)	$1 300
Cr. Accounts payable—Company B	$11 300
May 8, 2022	
Dr. Accounts payable—Company B	$11 300
Cr. Cash in bank	$11 300

5.3.2 Accounting for Fixed Assets Purchasing

Fixed assets are those long-lived assets acquired by a business for use in operations, rather than for resale to customers. Examples of such assets include land, buildings, equipment, machinery, and vehicles.

Fixed assets are expected to be used in the future to produce goods or services for sale to customers. Since they have value in use, they contain future service benefits for the business. For example, buildings contain future housing service benefits for the business, automobiles have future transportation services; and computers contain future data processing services.

The cost of a fixed asset includes all the expenditures necessary to obtain the asset to get it ready for the use intended by the purchaser. An expenditure is either a cash payment or liability incurred to acquire a good or service. For example, the cost of acquiring a machine includes its invoice price (minus any cash discounts), sales taxed, freight, insurance in transit, installation expenditures (such as power hookup), and any initial adjustments needed to make the machine function properly.

On June 5, 2022, Shanhai Company bought equipment C for $50 000 with the special VAT invoice of 13%, and installation expenditure was $900. Thus the total costs of equipment C were calculated as follows:

List price of equipment C	$50 000
Input VAT ($50 000x13%)	$6 500
Installation	$900
Total	$57 400

The journal entry was kept as the following:

June 5, 2022	
Dr. Fixed assets—equipment C	$50 900
Taxes and surcharges payable—VAT payable (input)	$6 500
Cr. Cash in bank	$57 400

If a note payable with the par value of $57 400 was issued to the seller by Shanhai Company, the entry was made as follows:

June 5, 2022	
Dr. Fixed assets—equipment C	$50 900
Taxes and surcharges payable—VAT payable (input)	$6 500
Cr. Notes payable	$57 400

5.4 Accounting of Production Process Business

The production process business (cost flow) associated with the manufacturing process used to convert raw materials into finished products causes more complicated accounting problems than those experienced by non-manufacturing business. In this section, we will learn the accounting process for manufacturing in a manufacturing business.

5.4.1 The flow of Manufacturing Cost

The different inventory accounts must be maintained by a manufacturing firm: Raw Materials, Work-in-Process, and Finished Goods. At the end of any accounting period, the balance in each of these three inventory accounts will be reported as a current asset on the balance sheet. A proper matching of revenue and expenses depends on the accuracy with which the costs of the three inventories are accounted for during the firm's production. Costs are transferred from raw materials to work-in-process to finished goods and, ultimately, to cost of goods sold. The three types of the inventory of manufacturing are the following.

Finished goods: The total cost recorded during the production process for all products fully manufactured and ready for sale is classified as the cost of finished goods inventory. For example, all the costs incurred to produce automobiles that have been completed but awaiting delivery to the manufacturer's dealers will be shown as finished goods.

Work-in-process: Inventory that is partially finished but requires further processing before it can be sold is classified as work-in-process inventory. For example, all the automobiles placed into production on an assembly line but unfinished at the end of an accounting period will be treated as work-in-process inventory.

Raw materials: The items acquired by purchase, growth (such as food products), or extraction (natural resources) for processing into finished goods are classified as raw mate rial inventory. Examples are the steel, aluminum, glass, zinc, rubber plastics, paint, and other basic ingredients used to manufacture automobiles. Such items are accounted for as raw material inventory until used. When used, their cost is included in the work-in-process inventory (along with other processing costs such as direct labor and manufacturing overhead). The flow of inventory costs in a manufacturing environment can be diagrammed as shown in Figure 5-2.

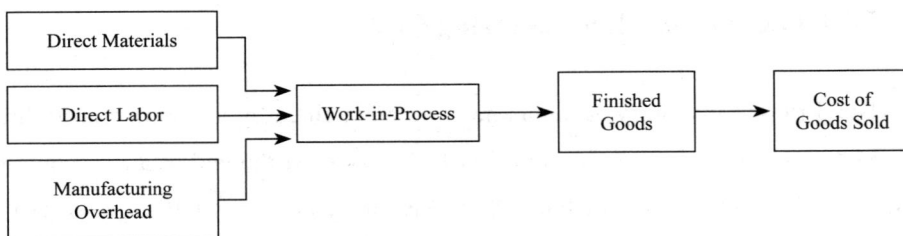

Figure 5-2 The flow of Manufacturing Costs

In accounting, items related to manufacturing cost are divided into three kinds: direct materials, direct labor, and manufacturing overhead.

Direct materials are those raw materials used in manufacturing which can be allocated directly to the products.

Direct labor refers to the manufacturing workers, whom the wages are paid and that can be allocated directly to the products.

Manufacturing overheads which different from direct materials and direct labor, which are all the other production expenditures that can not be allocated directly to the products' cost. They are indirectly paid for the organization and management in the manufacturing procedure. Such expenses are related to water and electricity, leasing, insurance of property, depreciation and so on.

The manufacturing cost flow can be illustrated as above (Figure 5-2).

In addition to accounting for production cost, accounting for manufacturing involves calculating the expenses which are distributed directly to an industry's profits and losses in a certain period. They are administrative expense, financial expense, sales expense, advertising expense, interest expense, etc. According to the above, major accounts designed in accounting for manufacturing belong to Costs (e.g. manufacturing cost and manufacturing overhead), Liabilities (e.g. payables to employees), Assets (e.g. finished goods and accumulated depreciation), Profit and Loss (e.g. administrative expense), etc. The formula of accounting for manufacturing can be illustrated as bellow.

Manufacturing Cost

= Direct Materials Cost + Direct Labor Cost + Manufacturing Overhead

Period Expenses

= Administrative Expenses + Financial Expenses + Sales Expenses

5.4.2 Calculation in Manufacturing Cost

We still take the Shanhai Company as example. The company rented respectively a plant and some offices for $8 000 and $4 000 per month to run the business. The company paid $36 000 for the rent of the first quarter on January 1, 2022.

Salaries and wages were paid once a month in this company. On January 28, 2022, the company paid $14 000 (all direct) for the manufacturing workers and $11 200 (non-manufacturing) for administrative staff.

The company also paid $3 500 for other manufacturing expenses on January 20, 2022.

The following entries were made:

Jan. 1, 2022	
Dr. Advances to suppliers—rent	$36 000
Cr. Cash in bank	$36 000
Jan. 20, 2022	
Dr. Manufacturing overhead	$3 500
Cr. Cash in bank	$3 500
Jan. 28, 2022	
Dr. Manufacturing cost—direct labor	$14 000
Administrative expenses—salaries	$11 200
Cr. Cash in bank	$25 200

Manufacturing costs were summarized at the end of the accounting period after the following related adjusting entries in Shanhai Company.

(1) Prepaid rent: The rent was paid at the beginning of the month for three months, partially for manufacturing and partially for administrative purposes. Only those, which were paid for manufacturing use and benefiting this accounting period, can be recorded as manufacturing cost of this month.

Jan. 31, 2022	
Dr. Manufacturing overhead	$8 000
Administrative expenses—rent	$4 000
Cr. Advances to suppliers—rent	$12 000

(2) Depreciation: The service benefits contained in fixed assets will be used for more than one accounting period, so the cost of the assets is allocated in a systematic manner to the accounting periods that benefit from their use. In other words, as the assets are used to produce the goods or services, their cost is transferred to depreciation expense to match it with the revenue produced by the sale of the goods or services. Here the matching principle is applied. The company spent $96 000 on the equipment at the beginning of January, so if the equipment was depreciated at an annual rate of 10%, the depreciation expense of this month was $800 (i.e. 96 000*10%÷12=800).

Jan. 31, 2022	
Dr. Manufacturing overhead	$800
Cr. Accumulated depreciation—machinery	$800

(3) Salaries and wages owed: If 28 days'salaries and wages in Shanhai Company had been paid in January, there were still 3 days'salaries and wages owed to the production workers and administrative staff. The owed should be also recorded as cost and expense in January according to the matching principle.

Jan. 31, 2022	
Dr. Manufacturing cost—direct labor ($14 000÷28×3)	$1 500
Administrative expenses—salaries ($11 200÷28×3)	$1 200
Cr. Payables to employees	$2 700

A period inventory system was used in Shanhai Company. At the beginning of the month, the inventory in Shanhai Company was zero, and raw materials worth $11 000 were purchased during the month. By the end of the month, the remaining raw materials in the warehouse worth $500 (all the materials were direct). After all the finished goods were moved to the warehouse, the unfinished goods (i.e. work in process) worth $800 (half were direct labor and half were raw materials, and manufacturing overhead was zero) were still in the workshop.

So in Shanhai Company we can see the following items in January, 2022.

Direct Materials Cost

= Beginning Direct Materials + New Purchase of this Period-Ending Direct Materials

= 0 + $11 000 − $500

= $10 500

Direct Labor Cost

= $14 000 + $1 500 (please refer to previous entries)

= $15 500

Manufacturing Overhead Cost

= $3 500 + $8 000 + $800 (please refer to previous entries)

= $12 300

Meanwhile, manufacturing overhead should be transferred to manufacturing cost.

Jan. 31, 2022	
Dr. Manufacturing cost	$12 300
Cr. Manufacturing overhead	$12 300

In this accounting period, the cost of goods manufactured can be computed as the following:

Cost of Goods Manufactured

= Direct Materials Cost + Direct Labor Cost + Manufacturing Overhead Cost + Beginning Inventory (Work in Process) − Ending Inventory (Work in Process)

= $10 500 + $15 500 + $12 300 + 0 − $800

= $37 500

After all the finished goods were moved into the warehouse for sale, the entry with the cost of $37 500 was made in Shanhai Company on January 31, 2022.

Jan. 31, 2022	
Dr. Finished goods	$37 500
Cr. Manufacturing cost	$37 500

5.5 Accounting of Sales Process Business

In an enterprise, selling its product means that the product's values and the operating results can be realized. During the selling course, sales revenue flows in, and both cost of sales and selling expense generate with the related tax payments. As a result, it's important for the enterprise to record properly its sales revenue and cost of goods sold, which is necessary for its managers and users of the financial statements. In order to conduct accounting practice and exercise accounting supervision on the selling matters, accounts on Profit and Loss and Assets shall be created for an enterprise. In Profit and Loss, accounts are prime operating revenue, other operating revenue, operating costs, other operating cost, tax and associate charges, selling expenses, etc. In assets, the account can be accounts receivable.

5.5.1 Accounting for Sales Revenue

Revenue is the gross inflow of economic benefits derived from the ordinary activities of selling products that result in increases in the owner's equity. However, revenue is recognized only when it is probable that economic benefits will flow to the enterprise, which will result in an increase in assets or a decrease in liabilities and the amount of the inflow of economic benefits can be measured reliably.

Sales revenue should be recorded at the right amount in appropriate accounting period. Sales may be for cash or on credit.

In most cases, the seller records sales revenue when the ownership of goods is passed from the seller to the buyer. Under the revenue principle, the sales price (net of any discount) is the measure of the amount of revenue that should be recorded. If the sale is for cash, the amount of revenue to be recorded is the amount of cash that is received. If the sale is on credit, the revenue is the cash equivalent of the assets to be received excluding any financing charges (i.e. , interest).

A large portion of the sales made by many businesses is on credit. When goods are sold on credit, the terms of payment should be definite so there will be no misunderstanding as to the amounts and due dates.

In 2022, Shanhai Company sold some toys at the price of $22 000 on January 15 and made another sale for $28 000 on January 25 with the amount of output VAT $2 860, $3 640 respectively. Half of the sales were for cash and half on credit with the credit term "n/30". Shanhai Company recognized the sales as follows.

Jan. 15, 2022	
Dr. Cash in bank	$12 430
Accounts receivable	$37 500
Cr. Prime operating revenue	$22 000
Taxes and surcharges payable—VAT payable (output)	$2 860
Jan. 25, 2022	
Dr. Cash in bank	$15 280
Accounts receivable	$15 280
Cr. Prime operating revenue	$28 000
Taxes and surcharges payable—VAT payable (output)	$3 640

Despite careful credit investigation, a few credit customers will not pay their bills. If a receivable account is uncollectible, the business will incur a bad debt expense. Businesses that extend credit know that there will be a certain amount of the bad debt losses on credit sales. Bad debt losses can be thought of as a necessary expense associated with generating credit sales.

In conformity with the matching principle, bad debt expense must be matched with the sales revenue that ever caused those losses. This requirement is difficult to implement because it may be in one or more accounting periods after the sales were ever made before the business knows that the customer will be unable to pay.

In China, to satisfy the matching principle, the bad debt allowance method is used to measure bad debt expense. The allowance method recognizes that bad debt expenses must be recorded in the period in which the sales that caused those losses were made rather than in the period that the customer is unable to pay. Therefore, the allowance method is based on estimates of the probable amount of bad debt losses from uncollectible accounts. The estimate is made in each accounting period based on either the total credit sales of the period or aging of accounts receivable.

Shanhai Company also used bad debt allowance method to record bad debt expenses. It recognized 5% of the ending balance of accounts receivable as the bad debt expense of that accounting period.

Jan. 31, 2022	
Dr. Credit impairment loss ($28 250×5%)	$1 412. 50
Cr. Bad debt allowance	$1 412. 50

5.5.2 Accounting for Cost of Goods Sold

Cost of goods sold (COGS) is a major expense item for most nonservice businesses and is directly related to sales revenue. It includes the cost of all products (or merchandise in commercial companies) sold during the same accounting period in which relative sales are made. The cost of products or merchandise remaining on hand at the end of the accounting period (i.e. the ending finished goods or merchandise inventory) is excluded from cost of goods sold. The measurement of cost of goods sold is an excellent example of the application of the matching principle.

During the accounting period, the beginning inventory (BI, also called the beginning balance of the goods) is increased by the manufacture or purchase of more goods. The sum of the beginning inventory and the newly increased finished goods (NFG) or purchase (P) during the period represents the goods available for sale during that period. If all the goods available for sale were sold during the period, there would be no ending inventory (EI, also called Ending balance of the goods). In fact, not all of the goods available for sale are sold, and there is an ending inventory in the period. From these relationships, we can compute cost of goods sold as follows:

$$COGS = BI + NFG \text{ (or P)} - EI$$

At the end of January, 2022, there remained finished goods worth $1 500 in Shanhai Company. In this period, BI was $0 and COGM (i.e. Cost of goods manufactured) was $37 500. To illustrate, Shanhai Company reported cost goods sold of $36 000, which was computed as follows.

Beginning inventory (Jan. 1, 2022)	0
Add: Cost of goods manufactured during Jan. 2022	$37 500
Goods available for sale	$37 500
Deduct: Ending inventory (Jan. 31, 2022)	$1 500
Result: Cost of goods sold	$36 000
So the related entry should be:	
Jan. 31, 2022	
Dr. Operating costs	$36 000
Cr. Finished goods	$36 000

5.6 Accounting for Financial Results

5.6.1 The Definition of Financial Results

Financial operating results are the final results of business operations and investment activities carried out by an enterprise in a certain accounting period. If the revenue achieved in the current period is greater than the related costs and expenses, it is a profit, and vice versa, it is a loss. According to China's current "Accounting Standards for Enterprises (2006)", the profits (non-operating income) and losses (non-operating expenses) generated by an enterprise in the current period should be directly included in the accounting period in which they occur. (Among them, profits will increase the profit of the current period, while losses will decrease the profit of the current period.)

The results of operations are formed by the organization and management of the business activities of the enterprise. However, the exact amount of profit realized or loss incurred needs to be recognized in accounting using certain methods. The final indicator of financial results recognized by the enterprise is the net profit (or net loss) of the enterprise. Therefore, mastering the calculation method and accounting method of net profit (net loss) should be the key content of the study of financial results.

5.6.2 Calculation in Financial Results

Financial results refer to the profits that a company makes in a certain accounting period, and are always classified into three types, namely operating profit, total profit and net profit, and in this book total profit is seen as the taxable item. The relationships among them can be shown as follows:

Total Profit = Operating Profit + Non-operating Income − Non-business Expenditure

Net Profit = Total Profit − Income Tax Expenses

Income Tax Expenses = Total Profit × Tax Ratio

In order to conduct accounting practice and supervision on a company's financial results, some specific accounts are designed. They are investment income, non-operating income, non-business expenditure, income tax expenses, income summary, etc. In the account of income summary, the amounts that should be entered on the credit side are from prime operating revenue, other operating revenue, investment income (net income) and non-operating income. On the other hand, the amounts recorded on the debit side result from operating costs, other operating costs, tax and associate charges, investment income (net loss), selling expenses, administrative expenses, financial expenses, non-business expenditure, and income tax expenses and so on. After the final calculation, the amount of balance on the credit side means the amount of net income that accrues in a certain accounting period. On the contrary, when the amount of balance appears on the debit side , it implies the amount of net loss.

Still we follow the illustration of Shanhai Company. In 2022, Calculations of operating profit, total profit and net profit for Shanhai Company are shown below.

Operating profit = $1 200 000 (prime operating revenue) + $100 000 (other operating revenue) − $600 000 (operating costs) − $40 000 (other operating cost) − $80 000 (administrative expenses) − $12 704. 80 (financial expenses) − $24 000 (selling expenses)

= $543 295. 20

Total profit = $543 295. 20 + $10 000 (non-operating income) − $1 000 (non-business expenditure)

= $552 295. 20

Net profit = $552 295. 20 − $138 073. 80 (income tax expenses) = $414 221. 40

Profit distribution means the distribution of a company's net income. It's mainly related to statutory surplus reserves drawn from the net income at the certain rate and the income distributed to investors of a company. Accounts concerning this process are profit distribution, surplus reserves and dividends payable.

On December 31, 2022, statutory surplus reserves was drawn from the net income at the rate of 10% and $100 000 of cash dividend was allotted as investors' income. Accounting personnel can enter the item of profit distribution as follows.

Dec. 31, 2022	
(1) Dr. Profit distribution—statutory surplus reserves ($414 221. 40×10%)	$41 422. 14
—Cash dividends	$100 000
Cr. Surplus reserves—statutory surplus reserves	$41 422. 14
Dividends payable	$100 000
(2) Dr. Profit distribution—unappropriated profits	$141 422. 14
Cr. Profit distribution—statutory surplus reserves	$41 422. 14
—Cash dividends	$100 000

Chapter 6   Adjusting Entries Before Closing Procedure

Learning Objectives:

(1) To learn to make basic entries of accounting practice.

(2) To command the calculation of financial results.

6.1 The Concept of Accrual Basis of Accounting

The income statement reports the operating performance of a business entity over a specified period. Thus, it is necessary to reflect revenue and expense items applicable to that period.

The cash basis of accounting recognizes revenues and expenses only when the related cash is received and disbursed. Thus, income statement recognition of transactions is tied to cash flow. Individuals and professionals generally use the cash basis as a measure of what they have earned for a given period. However, the cash basis is an inappropriate accounting method when considerable incongruence exists between cash inflows or outflows the time the company sells or purchases the related items.

Accrual basis (sometimes called accrual method): Under the accrual method, income is counted when the sale occurs, and expenses are counted when you receive the goods or services, regardless of when the money for them (receivables) is actually received or paid.

Under accrual accounting, revenue is recognized when earned and expenses are recorded when incurred. Most companies use the accrual basis accounting in accordance with generally accepted accounting principles (GAAP). Accrual basis accounting means that transactions that change a company's financial statements are recorded in the periods in which the events occur, rather than when the company actually receives or pays cash.

Inherent in the accrual method of accounting are the revenue recognition principle and the matching principle. The revenue recognition principle dictates that revenue should be recognized in the accounting period in which it is earned. In a service company, revenue is considered earned at the time the service is rendered. For example, assume a laundry business cleans clothing on October 30, but customers do not claim and pay for their clothes until the end of November. Under the revenue recognition principle, revenue is earned in October when the service is rendered, not in November when the cash is received. The matching principle states that expenses should be deducted against the revenue to which they are directly related. Thus, expense recognition is tied to revenue recognition. For example, the monthly rent paid for a store should be matched against the sales generated during that month. The accrual concept also requires the adjustment of income statement accounts at the end of a period to appropriately reflect the revenue earned and expenses incurred for that period.

Individuals and some small companies do use cash-basis accounting. The cash-basis is justified for small businesses because they often have few receivables and payables. Medium and large companies use accrual basis accounting.

Example: Accrual Basis Accounting

For the month of June, employees who are paid bi-weekly were last paid on June 27. They have since worked three additional days (June 28~June 30) but will not be paid until the next pay day, which comes in early July. Assuming that the wage for the three days totals $600, what should be done to properly reflect the wage expense for the month of July?

According to the accrual basis of accounting, the company should accrue an additional wage expense of $600 for the month of June to properly reflect the total wage expense for that month.

6.2 The End-of-Period Adjustments

6.2.1 Prepaid Accounts

Prepaid accounts are assets because they relate to expenditures made which have future economic benefits. Examples are prepaid insurance and prepaid rent. When a prepayment expires in a given accounting period, we are required to record the expired portion as an expense. Thus, prepaid expenses are items that have been prepaid but not incurred yet.

Prepaid accounts are initially recorded as an asset when paid and need to be adjusted at the end of an accounting period. Therefore, it has two journal entries involved: one at the time when paid and one at the end of an accounting period.

The journal entry at the time of payment would be as follows:

Dr. Prepaid Expense　　　　　　　　　　　　　×××

　　Cr. Cash　　　　　　　　　　　　　　　　　×××

The journal entry to adjust a prepaid expense to an actual expense for the period takes the following form:

Dr. Expense　　　　　　　　　　　　　　　　×××

　　Cr. Prepaid Expense　　　　　　　　　　　×××

Framework: Adjusting entries for prepaid increase expenses and decrease assets, as shown in the T-accounts. Such adjustments reflect transactions and events that use up prepaid expenses (including the passage of time). To illustrate the accounting for prepaid expenses, we look at prepaid insurance, supplies, and depreciation. In each case we decrease an asset (balance sheet) account and increase an expense (income statement) account.

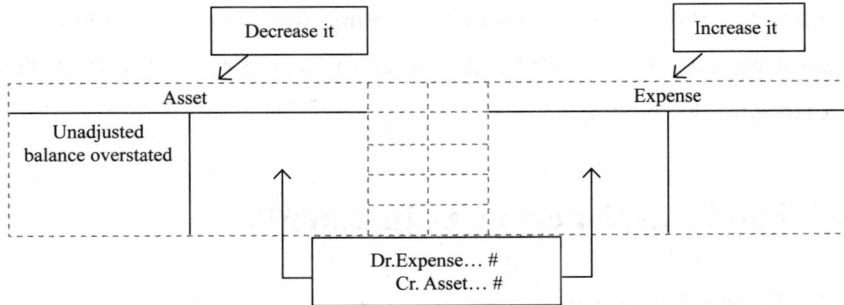

Figure 6-1 T-accounts for Adjusting Entries for Prepaids

Prepaid accounts are the advance payment of future expenses and are recorded as assets when cash is paid. Prepaid expenses become expenses over time or during normal operations. Examples are prepaid insurance, supplies, and other prepaid expenses.

Example—Prepaid Rent

On April 1, ABC Company, which prepares semi-annual financial statements on June 30 and December 31 respectively, paid $1 200 to the landlord for a one-year rent at the start of the rental agreement. This transaction was recorded on April 1 as an increase in the asset Prepaid Rent and a reduction in the asset Cash. The journal entry is:

April 1

Dr. Prepaid Rent $1 200

    Cr. Cash $1 200

On June 30, a quarter of the prepaid annual rent or $300 ($1 200×3/12) has expired and three quarters ($900) yet to expire. Therefore, we need to reflect the expired portion ($300) as expense and the unexpired portion ($900) as an asset. Note that the company recorded Prepaid Rent of $1 200 on April 1 when the annual rent was paid in advance. Therefore, it is required to decrease the asset by $300 so that the expired portion is reflected as expense during the period it was consumed or expired in accordance with the accrual basis of accounting. The adjusting entry requires a decrease in the account Prepaid Rent, which thus must be credited, and the recognition of Rent Expense which must be debited. This journal entry is:

June 30

Dr. Rent Expense $300

   Cr. Prepaid Rent $300

Rent Expense of $300 would be properly reflected in the semi-annual income statement for the period. The semi-annual statement of financial position as of June 30 would show Prepaid Rent of $900 as an asset.

6.2.2 Accrued Expenses

An accrued (unrecorded) expense is an expense that has been incurred at the end of the reporting period but has not been paid. Typical examples of accrued expenses include accrued interest expense, accrued rent expense, accrued salaries expense, accrued utilities expense, and others of similar nature.

An accrued expense requires an adjusting entry in the journal as follows:

Dr. Expense   ×××

   Cr. Payable   ×××

Accrued expenses are unrecorded expenses that have been incurred and for which cash has yet to be paid. Wages owed to employees at the end of a period but not yet paid is an accrued expense. Other examples of accrued expenses include accrued interest on notes payable and accrued taxes.

Framework: Adjusting entries for recording accrued expenses increases the expense (income statement) account and increases a liability (balance sheet) account. This adjustment recognizes expenses incurred in a period but not yet paid. We use salaries and interest to show how to adjust accounts for accrued expenses.

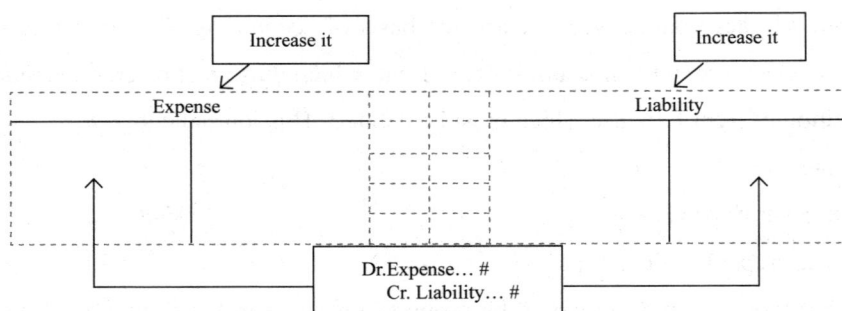

Figure 6-2　Adjusting Entries for Recording Accrued Expenses

Example—Accrued Rent Expense

Let's use the same example of rent expense with a slight modification. On April 1, 20 ×1, ABC Company, which prepares semi-annual financial statements on June 30 and December 31 respectively, entered into a rental agreement with the landlord under which ABC Company would pay $1 200 for a one-year rent at the end of the rental agreement, namely on March 31, 20×2. On June 30 when ABC Company prepares semi-annual financial statements, it has used the rented space for three months without paying the rent yet. ABC Company should accrue rent expense and rent payable of $300 so that related expense and liability would be properly measured and reflected in the semi-annual financial statements. This journal entry is:

June 30

Dr. Rent Expense　　　　　　　　　　　　　　　$300

　　Cr. Rent Payable　　　　　　　　　　　　　　$300

With this adjusting entry, rent expense of $300 would be properly reflected in the semi-annual income statement. The semi-annual statement of financial position as of June 30 would show rent payable of $300 as a liability. Without this adjusting entry, rent expense and rent payable would be understated.

6.2.3 Revenue Apportionment

Revenue apportionment refers to revenue received in advance. Since a future obligation exists on the part of the company to perform the services for which the advance payment was received, revenue apportionment constitutes a liability (Although a liability is usually thought of as an obligation requiring a future cash payment, it can also relate to the rendering of future services).

Just like prepaid expenses, revenue apportionments are recorded as a liability when received and later adjusted at the end of an accounting period. Therefore, when received, revenue apportionment is recorded as a liability as follows:

Dr. Cash   ×××

    Cr. Unearned Revenue   ×××

Later when the services are performed or time elapses, revenue is then earned and the following journal entry is required:

Dr. Unearned Revenue   ×××

    Cr. Revenue   ×××

Framework: As products or services are provided, the liability decreases, and the unearned revenues become earned revenues. Adjusting entries for unearned items decrease the unearned (balance sheet) account and increase the revenue (income statement) account.

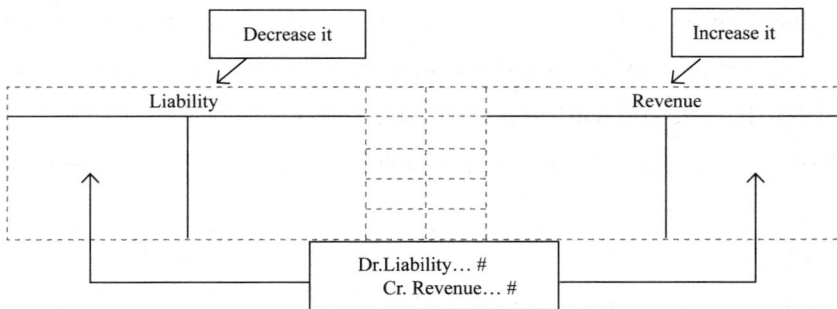

Figure 6-3 Adjusting Entries for Unearned Items

Revenue apportionments are the advance receipt of future revenues and are recorded as liabilities when cash is received. Unearned revenues become earned revenues over time or during normal operation. Examples are unearned rent, unearned tuition received in advance by a school, an annual retainer fee received by an attorney, premiums received in advance by an insurance company, and magazine subscriptions received in advance by a publisher.

Often, a business will collect monies in advance of providing goods or services. For example, a magazine publisher may sell a multi-year subscription and collect the full payment at or near the beginning of the subscription period. Such payments received in advance are initially recorded as a debit to Cash and a credit to unearned Revenue. Unearned revenue is reported as a liability, reflecting the company's obligation to deliver product in the future. Remember, revenue cannot be recognized in the income statement until the earnings process is complete.

Example—Unearned Rent Income

The tenant ABC Company paid $1 200 to the landlord for a one-year rent at the start of the rental agreement. Now, let's learn how the landlord should account for the rent at the time of receipt on April 1 and on June 30 assuming that the landlord also prepares semi-annual financial statements on June 30.

On April 1, the landlord would record $1 200 as a liability since the landlord has an obligation to provide the rental space to the tenant for one year period. Even though the landlord received cash on April 1, it is too early to recognize rental income since the landlord has not completed the service of providing the rental space to the tenant. That is why the landlord should record the receipt of cash as a liability on April 1 and will record rental income as time passes.

Therefore, the following journal entry will be made by the landlord on April 1:

April 1

Dr. Cash $1 200

    Cr. Unearned Rent Income $1 200

Then on June 30, when the landlord prepares semi-annual financial statements, the landlord has earned three-month rent income of $300 and the remaining $900 indicates the obligation that the landlord should provide in the remaining rental period of nine months. Therefore, the following adjusting entries should be made to properly measure revenue(rent income) and liability(unearned rent income):

June 30

Dr. Unearned Rent Income $300

    Cr. Rent Income $300

Just like the prepaid expense, the adjusting entry for unearned revenue is to adjust the already recorded liability (unearned rental income) so that you can properly measure related revenue (earned portion) and liability (unearned portion). Therefore, the adjusting entry for unearned revenue is also considered an alignment of recorded item.

6.2.4 Accrued Revenue

Accrued revenues are revenues earned in a period that are both unrecorded and not yet re ceived in cash (or other assets). An example is a technician who bills customers after the job is done. If one-third of a job is completed by the end of a period, then the technician must record one-third of the expected billing as revenue in that period-even though there is no billing or collection. The appropriate journal entry is:

Dr. Receivable   ×××

    Cr. Income   ×××

Framework: The adjusting entries for accrued revenues increase a revenue (income statement) account and increase an asset (balance sheet) account. Accrued revenues commonly arise from services, products, interest, and rent. We use service fees and interest to show how to adjust for accrued revenues.

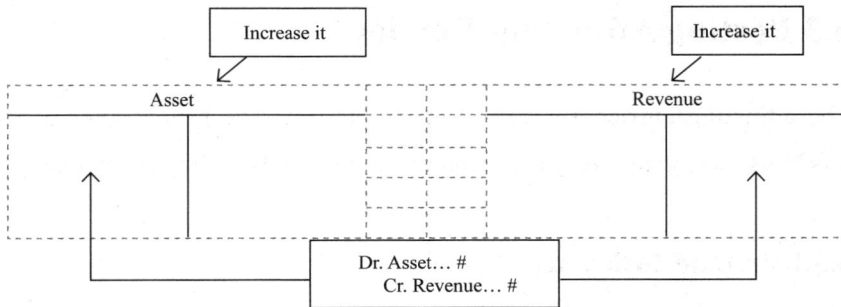

Figure 6-4　Adjusting Entries for Accrued Revenues

Accrued revenues are unrecorded revenues that have been earned and for which cash has yet to be received. Fees for services that an attorney or a doctor has provided but not yet billed are accrued revenues. Examples are accounts receivable, accrued interest on notes receivable and accrued rent on property rented to others.

Example—Accrued Rent Income

On April 1, 2021, the landlord, who prepares semi-amual financial statements on June 30 and December 31 respectively, entered into a rental agreement with a tenant under which the tenant would pay a one-year rent of $1 200 at the end of the rental agreement, namely on March 31, 2022. On June 30 when the landlord prepares the semi-annual financial statements, it has earned rent income for three months even though it has not received the rent yet. The landlord should accrue rent revenue and rent receivable of $300 so that related revenue and asset would be properly measured and reflected in the semi-annual financial statements. This journal entry is:

June 30

Dr. Rent Receivable $300

    Cr. Rent Income $300

With this adjusting entry, Rent Income of $300 would be properly reflected in the semi-annual income statement. The semi-annual statement of financial position as of June 30 would show Rent Receivable of $300 as an asset. Without this adjusting entry, rent income and rent receivable would be understated.

6.3 Posting Adjusting Entries

The adjusting entries are posted individually to the proper general ledger accounts immediately after they are recorded on the last day of the accounting period.

6.3.1 Prepaid Insurance

Insurance policies are usually purchased in advance. Cash is paid up front to cover a future period of protection. Assume a three-year insurance policy was purchased on January 1, 2022 , for $6 000. By December 31, 2022, $2 000 of insurance coverage would have expired (one of three years, or 1/3 of $6 000). The following entries would be needed to record the transaction on January 1 and the adjustment on December 31:

Jan. 1

Dr. Prepaid Insurance	$6 000
Cr. Cash	$6 000

(Prepaid a three-year policy)

Dec. 31

Dr. Insurance Expense	$2 000
Cr. Prepaid Insurance	$2 000

(Adjust prepaid insurance expired)

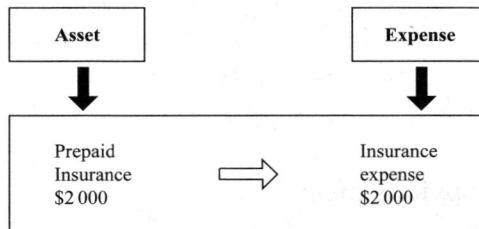

Figure 6-5　Prepaid Insurance Transaction

6.3.2 Supplies

The initial purchase of supplies is recorded by debiting Supplies and crediting Cash. Supplies Expense should subsequently be debited and Supplies credited for the amount used. This results in expense on the income statement being equal to the amount of supplies used, while the remaining balance of supplies on hand is reported as an asset. The following illustrates the purchase of $900 of supplies. Subsequently, $600 of this amount is used, leaving $300 of supplies on hand in the Supplies account:

May 1

Dr. Supplies $900

   Cr. Cash $900

(Purchase Supplies)

May 30

Dr. Supplies Expense $600

   Cr. Supplies $600

(Supplies used during the month)

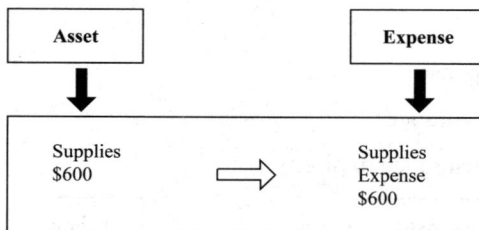

Figure 6-6   Supplies Transaction

6.3.3 Other Prepaid Expenses

Other prepaid expenses, such as Prepaid Rent, Prepaid Advertising, and Prepaid Promotions, are accounted for exactly as insurance and supplies are. Some prepaid expenses are both paid for and fully used up within a single accounting period. One example is when a company pays monthly rent on the first day of each month. This payment creates a prepaid expense on the first day of each month that fully expires by the end of the month. In these special cases, we can record the cash paid with a debit to an expense account instead of an asset account.

(1) Accrued interest: Most loans include charges for interest. The amount of interest therefore depends on the amount of the borrowing ("principal"), the interest

rate ("rate"), and the length of the borrowing period ("time"). The total amount of interest on a loan is calculated as Principal "Rate" Time. For example, if $100 000 is borrowed at 8% per year for 18 months, the total interest will amount to $12 000 ($100 000×8%×18/12). However, even if the interest is not payable until the end of the loan, it is still logical and appropriate to accrue the interest as time passes. This is necessary to assign the correct interest cost to each accounting period. Assume that an 18-month loan was taken out on July1, 2021, and was due on December 31, 2022. The accounting for the loan on the various dates (assume a December year end, with an appropriate year-end adjusting entry for the accrued interest) would be as follows:

Year 2021

Jul.	1	Cash	100 000	
		Loan payable		100 000
		Borrow $100 000 at 8% per year and interest due on Dec. 12, 2022		

Dec.	31	Interest expense	4 000	
		Interest payable		4 000
		Accured interest for six months		

Year 2022

Dec.	31	Interest expense	8 000	
		Interest payable	4 000	
		Loan payable	100 000	
		Cash		112 000
		Repayment of loan interest		

(2) Accrued rent: Accrued rent is the opposite of prepaid rent discussed earlier. Recall that prepaid rent related to rent that was paid in advance. In contrast, accrued rent relates to the rent that has not yet been paid, even though use of the asset has already occurred. For example, assume that office space is leased, and the terms of the agreement state that rent will be paid within 10 days after the end of each month

at the rate of $400 per month, from December 1, 2021 to June 30, 2022. During December of 2021, ABC Company occupied the lease space, and the appropriate adjusting entry for December follows:

Dec.	31	Rent Expense		400	
		Rent payable			400
		To record accrued rent			

When the rent is paid on January 10, 2022, this entry would be needed:

Jan.	10	Rent payable		400	
		Cash			400
		To record payment of accrued rent			

After adjusting entries are posted to general ledger accounts, a new balance is computed for each account. For an account with a debit balance, such as Office Supplies, the credit entry reduces the debit balance in the account. If the accounts are not in balance, an error in recording or posting the closing entries is indicated. The post-closing trial balance shows only assets, liabilities, and stockholders' equity accounts. As with any other posting, a new balance is computed at the same time the debit or credit entry is made.

As you can see, the new balances in these general ledger accounts are now the same as shown in the Adjusted Trial Balance columns of the worksheet.

6.4 TB Worksheet

An unadjusted trial balance is a list of accounts and balances prepared before adjustments are recorded. An adjusted trial balance is a list of accounts and balances prepared after adjusting entries have been recorded and posted to the ledger.

Exhibit 6-1 shows both the unadjusted and the adjusted trial balances for FastForward at December 31, 2021. The order of accounts in the trial balance usually matches the order in the chart of accounts. Several new accounts usually arise from adjusting entries.

Exhibit 6-1 FAETFORWARD

Acct. No.	Account title	Unadjusted Trail Balance Dr.	Unadjusted Trail Balance Cr.	Adjustments Dr.	Adjustments Cr.	Ajusted Trial Balance Dr.	Ajusted Trial Balance Cr.
		Trial Balances December 31, 2021					
101	Cash	$4 275				$4 275	
106	Accounts receivable	0		(f) $1, 800		1 800	
126	Supplies	9 720			(b) $1 050	8 670	
128	Prepaid insurance	2 400			(a) 100	2 300	
167	Equipment	26 000				26 000	
168	Accumulated derpreciation-Equip		$ 0		(b) 300		$300
201	Accounts payable		6 200				6 200
209	Salaries payable		0		(e) 210		210
236	Unearned consulting revenue		3 000	(d) 250			2 750
301	C. Taylor, Capital		30 000				30 000
302	C. Taylor, Withdrawls	200				200	
403	Consulting revenue		5 800		(d) 250		6 050
					(f) 1 800		1 800
406	Rental revenue		300				300
612	Depreciation expense-Equip	0		(c) 300		300	
622	Salaries expense	1 400		(e) 210		1 610	
637	Insurance expense	0		(a) 100		100	
640	Rent expense	1 000				1 000	
652	Supplies expense	0		(b) 1 050		1 050	
690	Untilities expense	305				305	
	Totals	$45 300	$45 300	$3 710	$3 710	$47 610	$47 610

Each adjustment (see middle columns) is identified by a letter in parentheses that links it to an adjusting entry explained earlier. Each amount in the Adjusted Trial Balance columns is computed by taking that account's amount from the Unadjusted Trial Balance columns and adding or subtracting any adjustment(s). To illustrate, Supplies has a $9 720 Dr. Balance in the unadjusted columns. Subtracting the $1 050 Cr. Amount shown in the Adjustments columns yields an adjusted $8 670 Dr. Balance for Supplies. An account can have more than one adjustment, such as for Consulting Revenue. Also, some accounts might not require adjustment for this period, such as Accounts Payable.

Exercise

TRUE/FALSE

(1) Deferrals are recorded transactions that delay the recognition of an expense or revenue.

(2) Adjustment for accruals are needed to record a revenue that has been earned or an expense that has been incurred but not recorded.

(3) The difference between the balance of a fixed asset account and the balance of its related accumulated depreciation account terms the book value of the asset.

(4) Accumulated Depreciation accounts are liability accounts.

(5) A building was purchased for $75 000. Assuming annual depreciation of $2,500, the book value of the building one year later is $77 500.

(6) A contra asset account for Land will normally appear in the balabce sheet.

(7) If the adjustment for accrued salaries at the end of the period is inadvertently omitted, both liabilities and owner's equity will be overstated for the period.

Answer: T T T F F F F

MULTIPLE CHOICE

(1) The adjusting entry to record the depreciation of equipment for the fiscal period is:

　　a. debit Depreciation Expense; credit Equipment

　　b. debit Depreciation Expense; credit Accumulated Depreciation

　　c. debit Accumulated Depreciation; credit Depreciation Expense

　　d. debit Equipment; credit Depreciation Expense

(2) The entry to adjust the accounts for wages accrued at the end of the accounting period is:

　　a. Wages Payable, debit; Wages Income, credit

　　b. Wages Income, debit; Wages Payable, credit

　　c. Wages Payable, debit; Wages Expense, credit

　　d. Wages Expense, debit; Wages Payable, credit

(3) The supplies account has a balance of $1 000 at the beginning of the year and was debited during the year for $2 800, representing the total of supplies purchased during the year. If $750 of supplies are on hand at the end of the year, the supplies expense to be reported on the income statement for the year is:

　　a. $750

　　b. $3 550

　　c. $3 800

　　d. $3 050

(4) A company purchases a one-year insurance policy on June 1 for $840. The adjusting entry on December 31 is:

　　a. debit Insurance Expense, $350 and credit Prepaid Insurance, $350

　　b. debit Insurance Expense, $280 and credit Prepaid Insurance, $280

　　c. debit Insurance Expense, $490, and credit Prepaid Insurance, $490.

d. debit Prepaid Insurance, $720, and credit Cash, $720

(5) Depreciation Expense and Accumulated Depreciation are classified, respectively, as:

a. expense, contra asset

b. asset, contra liability

c. revenue, asset

d. contra asset, expense

(6) The type of account and normal balance of Unearned Rent is:

a. revenue, credit

b. expense, debit

c. liability, credit

d. liability, debit

(7) Data for an adjusting entry described as "accrued wages, $2 020" means to debit:

a. Wages Expense and credit Wages Payable

b. Wages Payable and credit Wages Expense

c. Accounts Receivable and credit Wages Expense

d. Drawing and credit Wages Payable

Answer: b d d c a a a

Chapter 7　Errors and Suspense Accounts

7.1 Types of Errors

There are five main types of errors. Some can be corrected by a journal entry, some require the use of a suspense account. It is not really possible to draw up a complete list of all the errors which might be made by bookkeepers and accountants. It is possible to describe five types of errors which cover most of the errors which might occur. They are as follows: Errors of transposition, Errors of omission, Errors of principle, Errors of commission, Compensating errors.

Once an error has been detected, it needs to be put right. If the correction involves a double entry in the ledger accounts, then it is done by using a journal entry in the journal. When the error breaks the rule of double entry, then it is corrected by the use of a suspense account as well as a journal entry.

(1) Errors of transposition: An error of transposition is when two digits in an amount are accidentally recorded the wrong way round.

(2) Errors of omission: An error of omission means failing to record a transaction at all, or making a debit or credit entry, but not the corresponding double entry.

(3) Errors of principle: An error of principle involves making a double entry in the belief that the transaction is being entered in the correct accounts, but subsequently finding out that the accounting entry breaks the "rules" of an accounting principle or concept.

A typical example of such an error is to treat certain revenue expenditure incorrectly as capital expenditure.

(4) Errors of commission: Errors of commission are where the bookkeeper makes a mistake in carrying out his or her task of recording transactions in the accounts.

(5) Compensating errors: Compensating errors are errors which are, coincidentally, equal and opposite to one another.

Errors of transposition, Errors of omission (if the omission is one-sided), Errors of commission (if one-sided, or two debit entries are made, for example) can be detected by a trial balance.

Other errors will not be detected by extracting a trial balance, but may be spotted by other controls (such as bank or control account reconciliations).

7.2 Errors That Don't Affect TB Balance

(1) Errors of omission: Here is an example: If a business receives an invoice from a supplier for $200, the transaction might be omitted from the books entirely. As a result, both the total debits and the total credits of the business will be out by $200. So it will not affect TB balance.

(2) Errors of principle: A typical example of such an error is to treat certain revenue expenditure incorrectly as capital expenditure. For example, repairs to a machine costing $450 should be treated as revenue expenditure, and debited to a repairs account. If, instead, the repair costs are added to the cost of the non-current asset (capital expenditure), an error of principle would have occurred. As a result, although the repairs account is $450 less than it should be and the cost of the non-current asset is $450 greater than it should be, total debits still equal total credits.

(3) Errors of commission: Here are two common types of errors of commission.

① Putting a debit entry or a credit entry in the wrong account. For example, if telephone expenses of $570 are debited to the electricity expenses account, an error of commission would have occurred. The result is that although total debits and total credits balance, telephone expenses are understated by $570 and electricity expenses are overstated by the same amount.

② Errors of casting (adding up). The total daily credit sales in the sales day book should be $29 425, but are incorrectly added up as $29 825. The total sales in the sales day book are then used to credit total sales and debit total receivables in the ledger accounts. Although total debits and total credits are still equal, they are incorrect by $400.

(4) Compensating errors: For example, two transposition errors of $540 might occur in extracting ledger balances, one on each side of the double entry. In the administration expenses account, $2 282 might be written instead of $2 822, and in the sundry income account, $8 391 might be written instead of $8 931. Both the debits and the credits would be $540 too low, and the mistake would not be apparent when the trial balance is cast. Consequently, compensating errors hide the fact that there are ermors in the trial balance.

7.3 Errors That Do Affect TB Balance

(1) Errors of transposition: For example, suppose that a sale is recorded in the sales account as $5 843, but it has been incorrectly recorded in the total receivables account as $5 483. The error is the transposition of the 4 and the 8. The consequence is that total debits will not be equal to total credits. You can usually detect transposition errors by checking whether the debit is equal to the credit.

(2) Errors of omission: For example: If a business receives an invoice from a supplier for $300, the payables control account might be credited, but the debit entry in the purchases account might be omitted. In this case, the total credits would not equal total debits (because total debits are $300 less than they ought to be).

7.4 Correction of Errors

Errors which leave total debits and credits in the ledger accounts in balance can be corrected by using journal entries. Otherwise a suspense account has to be opened first, and later cleared by a journal entry.

Some errors can be corrected by journal entries. To remind you, the format of a journal entry is:

Date	Debit	Credit
	$	$
Account to be debited	X	
Account to be credited		X

(Narrative to explain the transaction)

The journal requires a debit and an equal credit entry for each "transaction", i.e. for each correction. This means that if total debits equal total credits before a journal entry is made then they will still be equal after the journal entry is made. This would be the case if, for example, the original error was a debit wrongly posted as a credit and vice versa.

Similarly, if total debits and total credits are unequal before a journal entry is made, then they will still be unequal (by the same amount) after it is made.

For example, a bookkeeper accidentally posts a bill for $40 to the local taxes account instead of to the electricity account. A trial balance is drawn up, and total debits are $40 000 and total credits are $40 000. A journal entry is made to correct the misposting error as follows.

DEBIT	Electricity account	$40
CREDIT	Local taxes account	$40

A misposting of $40 from the local taxes account to electricity account is corrected.

After the journal has been posted, total debits will still be $40 000 and total credits will be $40 000. Total debits and totals credits are still equal.

Now suppose that, because of some error which has not yet detected, total debits were originally \$40 000 but total credits were \$39 900. If the same journal correcting the \$40 is put through, total debits will remain \$40 000 and total credits will remain \$39 900. Total debits were different by \$100 before the journal, and they are still different by \$100 after the journal.

This means that journal can only be used to correct errors which require both a credit and (an equal) debit adjustment.

References

[1] Glautier C. Basic Accounting Practice[M]. New York: Pitman, 1978.

[2] Donald E, Kieso, Jerry J. Weygandt. Intermediate Accounting[M]. New York: John Wiley & Sons, Inc. 1992.

[3] Charles T Horngren, Gary L Sundem, John A Elliott. Introduction to Financial Accounting [M]. Upper Saddle River: Prentice Hall, 1996.

[4] Robert N Anthony, Leslie K Pearlman. Essentials of Accounting: 11 Edition[M]. 北京：清华大学出版社, 2001.

[5] 劳伦斯, 赖恩. 会计基础：影印版 [M]. 上海：立信会计出版社, 2003.

[6] 威廉·鲁兰德. 会计基本原理：影印版 [M]. 上海：立信会计出版社, 2003.

[7] Carl S Warren. Survey of Accounting[M]. 北京：高等教育出版社, 2004.

[8] Jan R Williams, Susan F Haka, Mark S Bettner. Financial and Managerial Accounting: 13 Edition[M]. 北京：机械工业出版社, 2005.

[9] 程淮中. 会计职业基础 [M]. 5 版. 北京：高等教育出版社, 2022.

[10] Collin. An English-Chinese Dictionary of Accounting[M]. 唐运冠, 译. 北京：外语教学与研究出版社, 2013.

[11] 于久洪. 会计英语 [M]. 5 版. 北京：中国人民大学出版社, 2021.

[12] 张其秀. 会计英语——财务会计：双语版. [M]. 4 版. 上海：上海财经大学出版社, 2021.